D1612663

By Candlelight

Non Omnis Moriar

(I shall not all die)

Inscription hung beneath his
portrait in the Ventnor Hospital
now at the entrance to the
Hassall Ward, Newport Hospital,
Isle of Wight

'In those days people often said to me, "Ah! the
microscope is all very well as an amusement,
but of what practical use is it in life?" these
people little dreaming of the many and vastly
important facts which in the future were to be
brought to light by its instrumentality.'

From *The Narrative of a Busy Life*, an autobiography by Arthur Hill Hassall, 1893.

By Candlelight

The life of
Dr Arthur Hill Hassall,
1817–94

Father of Modern Sanitary Science

Founder of the Ventnor Hospital for Consumption

Author of *A History of British Freshwater Algae*, etc

by

ERNEST A. GRAY

ROBERT HALE · LONDON

© *Ernest A. Gray 1983*

First published in Great Britain 1983

ISBN 0 7090 0922 4

Robert Hale Limited
Clerkenwell House
Clerkenwell Green
London, EC1

Photoset by Rowland Phototypesetting Ltd
Printed in Great Britain by St Edmundsbury Press,
Bury St Edmunds, Suffolk and
bound by Hunter & Foulis Ltd

Contents

Illustrations

Plates

Between pages 64 and 65

Arthur Hill Hassall aged about 45 (*Wellcome Institute Library, London*)

The chemist's shop, Cheshunt, possible site of Richard Hassall's apothecary establishment (*Cheshunt Public Library*)

Portrait of a Regency lady (*photo: Ramsey & Muspratt, Cambridge*)

Norland Villa, Addison Road North, London (*Kensington and Chelsea Public Libraries*)

Two herbarium sheets from Hassall's collection of British freshwater algae at the British Museum (*Trustees of the British Museum*)

One of Hassall's plates of pollen grains, drawn from his own sketches (*University Library, Cambridge*)

The Ventnor Hospital (*Tom Bryan*)

Arthur Hill Hassall aged about 62 (*Wellcome Institute Library, London*)

Portrait of Hassall by Lance Calkin (*Newport Hospital*)

Illustrations in the text

Five illustrations to Hassall's *Catalogue of Irish Zoophytes*, 1840–41, and facsimile page from the catalogue   pp 46–51

London's Drinking Water in 1851: three of Hassall's drawings with the Camera Lucida (*University Library, Cambridge*)   pp 92–3

Preface

As with John Hunter, so it is difficult to give Hassall a label; he was a remarkable pioneer in many fields. The pencil of light streaming through the lenses of his Ross microscope like a searching laser beam revealed how fungi might destroy fruit and vegetables three years before the Great Famine followed failure of the Irish potato crop, although his letters to the Press pointing out the cause were ignored; revealed the famous thymic corpuscles called after him and familiar to generations of veterinary and medical students, now the object of intense research since the discovery they are a seat of immunity; and detected the vibrio of cholera. A Senior Physician at the Royal Free Hospital, where a ward has lately been named in his honour, he founded the hospital for consumption at Ventnor on the open or cottage system; it continues to function at a special Hassall Ward of the Newport Hospital, Isle of Wight.

His greatest gift to us, however, has been the purity of everything we eat and drink. The wholesale adulteration of food and pollution of water the laser beam disclosed was under no control when he first turned his microscope on the problem. Well might the *Quarterly Review* exclaim, 'Nor does the daylight, when you lift a stone, startle ugly and loathsome things more quickly than the light streaming through a quarter-inch lens surprise in their native ugliness the thousand and one things which enter into every article of food.' Sir Edward Chadwick used Hassall's reports as ammunition to force a Public Health policy to the front. All subsequent legislation, from the first anti-adulteration Food Bill of 1860, the formation of the Local Government Board of 1871, the Act of 1875 that empowered local authorities to provide public and private water supplies, and so forth, stems directly from Hassall's pioneer researches, and the leaven is still working.

In 1851 he was chief witness at a Parliamentary Committee

of Enquiry into the Metropolitan Water Supply; and a year after his death, his widow, writing to the Earl of Rosebery, Premier, placed first among the labours that had earned for her husband the title of public benefactor, 'the researches and investigations which were the means of procuring a new water supply for London'. How that was accomplished was the life work of Joseph Bazalgette, chief engineer to the Metropolitan Board of Works that came into existence in 1855.

ONE
Peaches and Pestilence

Arthur Hill Hassall was born at Teddington, Middlesex, on 13 December 1817. His father was a surgeon and in due course he became a doctor practising in London for the first half of his life.

He was also a superb practical microscopist, certain of whose studies made with a Ross microscope were directly responsible for the first Food Adulteration Act of 6 August 1860, while his *Microscopic Anatomy of the Human Body* first published in 1852 was the first complete book in the English language on the subject, and is recalled today by the thymic corpuscles he described now known by his name. He was well known also as a zoologist and a botanist whose *History of the British Freshwater Algae* (first published in 1845) is an acknowledged classic.

Despite all these accomplishments he tells us that 'success in my profession was my chief aim and desire.' He so far attained this ambition as to become a Senior Physician at the Royal Free Hospital and in 1868 founded a famous hospital for consumption at Ventnor, Isle of Wight, which for a great many years had an international reputation.*

He practised under conditions difficult to grasp today, despite one illuminating glimpse. In 1849 when he was in practice at Addison Road North, Notting Hill, 'being in great pain from pleurisy I summoned my assistant Mr Collins in the middle of the night to bleed me . . . he was very pale and his hand shook . . . so I took the lancet from him and by the light of a candle bled myself.' This extract from his autobiography sets the stage of his life and labours, the dim dirty candle-lit world of Dickens' London where his patients were the originals of Dickens' immortal characters and the fog theme of Dickens' novel *Bleak House* was an appropriate symbol of a metaphorical fog in which

---

* The Royal National Hospital for Consumption changed its name by Royal Charter about 1950, dropping Consumption and substituting Diseases of the Chest.

at that time not simply the legal profession of the story, but in another context the medical profession too, and biology, floundered. Arthur's remarkable pioneer studies that made him a household word during his lifetime can only be appreciated at their true worth when viewed against the sinister vapour that in his day shrouded the cause of decay and infectious disease in profound obscurity.

He was the Benjamin of his family, the youngest of the five children of Thomas and Ann Hassall. He had two sisters Ann and Eliza, and two brothers. Richard, born on 12 June 1812, was five years older than he and also became a doctor. The eldest son, Arthur tells us – he does not mention his Christian name – 'being of an adventurous disposition, chose the sea, went out in a merchant vessel and never returned; the captain reported he had deserted his ship and was drowned in the attempt to reach another vessel. The account given was so unsatisfactory my father was fully persuaded there had been foul play, although of this he could never get clear and conclusive evidence. In those days great cruelties were often practised on merchant ships.'

Arthur never knew his mother. She died aged thirty-seven three days after he was born and was buried on 22 December 1817, presumably in the graveyard and not within the walls of St Mary's, the former parish church of Teddington. Her name is spelt without a terminal 'e' in both the baptism and burial register. It must have been a tragic Christmas for the little family suddenly made motherless, and a disaster that Ann bore four children uneventfully only to die at the birth of a fifth whose features suggest he was possibly the most sensitive, certainly it would seem the most artistic of them all, while he was deprived of the warm companionship often marked between a mother and her youngest son.

Thomas Hassall appears on Arthur's baptismal certificate as Surgeon. He was in practice at Teddington, Hampton Court and the neighbourhood.

Although Hassall is one of those surnames taken from a place,[1] in this instance in Cheshire, he was a Durham man whose own father was a surgeon practising at Sunderland.

Arthur's mother had a sister who married Sir James Murray, M.D., and Richard's obituaries[2] state he had an uncle Richard, presumably a brother-in-law of his father, also a medical man, and thus the Hassall family appear to have had a strong predilection for the medical profession. Arthur and Richard were keeping up the tradition.

The Durham Hassalls were related by marriage to the Strakers, Coppins and Sandersons, 'families well known in the north of England,' Arthur remarks. On one occasion while he was studying medicine at Dublin, he visited relatives at North Shields, and mentions that 'the family consisted of my cousin Mrs Coppin who was a Miss Hassall, her son and my life-long friend John Coppin, and my aunt Mrs Sanderson, who was a sister of my father.'

The Strakers owned coal-mines in Co. Durham but there are no detailed family histories of them, or of the Coppins or Sandersons.[3] John Coppin, Arthur's friend, of whom more will be heard later, was a barrister, a graduate of Trinity College, Cambridge.

Arthur must be mistaken, however, when he goes on to state that 'Mr Burdon-Sanderson secured for my father the double commission of Surgeon and Captain in the Durham Fencibles.' His father was commissioned in 1795, and Rowland Burdon was M.P. for Durham from 1790–1806. Burdon-Sanderson was born in Newcastle on Tyne in 1791, plain Richard Burdon until he married the daughter of Sir James Sanderson in 1815 and took the name Sanderson in addition to his own.

Rowland Burdon, M.P., of Castle Eden was responsible for the magnificent bridge over the Wear at Sunderland, the largest single arch cast-iron bridge in England. After it was opened in 1796 Sunderland rapidly expanded from a petty port and fishing village to its present importance. The Sunderland connection possibly explains how Thomas, whose father practised there, came to receive a commission.

The Fencibles were raised in England and Scotland for service in these islands during the war with France, and the volunteer Loyal Durham Regiment of Fencible Infantry served in Ireland during the rebellion of 1798.

Thomas Hassall was commissioned as Lieutenant and Surgeon on the 26 February 1795, the date on which the majority of the officers received theirs.[4] He may have been promoted later. They wore a uniform of the normal pattern for line infantry at that date, a scarlet frock coat with cuffs and lapels of contrasting colour, white breeches and a black tricorne hat.

Colonel John Skerrett succeeded to command of the Durham Fencibles in January 1798. At the time of his appointment, they had been at Downpatrick for six months after a spell of fifteen months (February 1796–May 1797) in Guernsey.[5]

'It was in Ireland,' Arthur writes, 'that my father first saw the young lady who was to become his wife. It was a case of "love at first sight." He was standing on the steps of a hotel in Downpatrick when a ladies' school passed; he was struck with the appearance of one of the young ladies, boldly made himself known to the mistress of the school, and after due enquiry and the necessary preliminaries the lady, a Miss Ann Sherrock, became Mrs Thomas Hassall.'

Thomas was seventy-three when he died a year or two after Arthur began practice in 1842 at Addison Road. We are not told the exact year, and the register of his burial has not been traced (see note at end of chapter). Assuming that he died in 1844 then he was born in 1771 and he would have been twenty-seven when he met Ann, and she eighteen.

Not long afterwards the Durhams greatly distinguished themselves at the Battle of Arklow, and he received a wound that cost him the sight of one eye. The Durhams had already acquired a formidable reputation in Ulster, and at Arklow one of three large rebel columns advancing on Dublin was opposed by a scratch Government force penned up in the town with their backs to the River Avoca and a single narrow bridge their only line of retreat. The Durhams arrival brought the Government strength up to some 1350 all ranks, opposed by between 20,000 and 30,000 rebels. The brunt of the fight that ensued fell on the Durhams whose Colonel Skerrett proved the hero of the hour. Thomas may have been wounded when a shot from a cannon laid by the rebel leader Kynan 'smashed the carriage of one of the six-pounder battalion guns supporting the Durhams and killed thirteen of the gun crew and troops who stood by.'[6]

Arklow was fought on the afternoon of 9 June and Arthur vividly recalled how on that never-to-be forgotten anniversary his father quoted with emphasis and pride 'a paragraph from some well-known historian of the time, to the effect that the conduct of the Durham Fencibles, in intercepting the march of the rebels on Dublin with a view to sack the city, had been the salvation of Ireland, if not of the British Empire.'

The Durhams arrived too late to take part at Vinegar Hill, the last battle of all. Thomas and Ann had an ugly experience there.

'At Vinegar Hill my father and mother had a narrow escape from being killed as they were out one day driving. They were about to be attacked under the idea that they were Protestants, but the rebels seeing my mother was wearing a green veil, came to the conclusion that they must belong to the Catholic party and hence their lives were spared.' Thomas must have been wearing civilian dress, for at sight of uniform of the hated Durhams particularly, green veil or no they would have instantly been piked to death.

The Durhams remained in Ireland until March or April 1802 and were disbanded at Liverpool on 22 May that year with a strength of 470 men. Their tradition became a heritage of the Durham Light Infantry.[5] The officers were offered commissions in the regular army, and Thomas obtained the post of Surgeon to the 1st Surrey Militia through the action of Lord Arthur Hill, held it for thirty years and finally retired on two pensions that brought in about £200 a year; one for length of service, and one awarded long afterwards for his Arklow wound by Lord Palmerston. He was at the War Office between 1809 and 1815, so the pension was probably awarded at some time during those years.

To mark his appreciation of his Militia Commission, Thomas bestowed the Christian names of Arthur Hill on his youngest son when he was baptised on 10 January 1818 at St Mary's, then the parish church of Teddington. Closed after nine hundred years of service in 1896, when St Alban's built on the opposite side of the road became the parish church, it was re-opened as a Chapel of Ease in 1930 (see note at end of chapter).

While Thomas practised in Teddington, the Duke of Clarence, afterwards William IV, was in residence at Bushey House with the Misses Clarence.

'On the suicide of His Royal Highness's resident medical attendant,' Arthur writes, 'my father in the absence of the

Duke was hurriedly summoned to Clarence House by Miss Fitzclarence. The Misses Fitzclarence were pleased with my father and he was for a time in attendance; they were most kind and condescending to him. A carriage was daily sent for him as he was himself not too well and occasionally he was asked to afternoon tea. My father happened to mention on one occasion that the tea had done him more good than all the medicines in the Pharmacopoeia; shortly afterwards the Misses Fitzclarence left Bushey Park temporarily and forwarded him before leaving a bag of the same tea, which he said had done him so much good.'

They further promised to secure him the post of Medical attendant to the Household. Unfortunately the Duke was not aware that he had been in attendance and had already appointed Mr, later Sir, Herbert Taylor to the post. Years later Arthur set out from Kew with his father, who had been reluctantly persuaded to approach Miss Fitzclarence, then Lady Sidney, on his behalf, since she had offered to be of service in the future. There was a hitch, they never got to London, nor could his father ever again be induced to make the effort.

Of his boyhood, Arthur observes, 'One source of regret is that my early training and education were so interrupted and limited and in many respects wanting in thoroughness,' and again, 'on the whole my education left much to be desired and it terminated earlier than usual from lack of funds and just as I was beginning to take an interest in acquiring knowledge for its own sake.'

It is difficult to reconcile these statements with the facts. When he was old enough to go to a boys' school, his father left Teddington for Kew Road, Richmond, and he had moved to another house at Richmond, in the Vineyard, when Arthur sailed for Ireland in 1834 to start his medical studies. Two moves in seventeen years scarcely suggest serious interruption. Five years later, in 1839 when Arthur was cramming for his M.R.C.S., and his school days were long since over, his father was at Upper Bedford Place, Kensington. He left to join Richard at Cheshunt, Hertfordshire, and when he returned to Richmond to start a practice,[7] went to live with Arthur at Addison Road, where he died about 1844. Arthur does not make it clear exactly when he did retire. 'On my father's retirement from practice at Teddington we went to reside at Richmond' might mean either that he exchanged practice at Teddington for Richmond, or gave it up altogether.

There is good evidence that the first assumption is the correct one. The candidate's entry qualification books of the Society of Apothecaries state that Richard Hassall was apprenticed to his father 'Thomas Hassall of Teddington, surgeon and apothecary' for five years in indenture dated 4 May 1827.[8] Richard would then be fifteen years old and the whole point of apprenticeship was to teach students the practical side of their business before they 'walked a hospital' for a few months and took their examinations. There would be no sense in apprenticing Richard if his father had already retired or was about to do so. When his indentures expired in 1832, only two years before Arthur sailed to Ireland to begin his own apprenticeship, the family were at Richmond. And when his father did at last retire, there should have been no serious shortage of money, since his pensions brought in £200 a year, worth a great deal more then than today. The fact that the Misses Fitzclarence sent a carriage for him suggests he did not keep one of his own but lived modestly and went his rounds on foot.

Arthur has a remarkable story about Richard. 'My second brother Richard did not till somewhat later adopt any profession; in fact, owing to my father's then very narrow resources, he was unable to do so, but my brother was nevertheless determined to make an independent position for himself. To that end he taught himself astronomy and chemistry and prepared a course of lectures on these subjects adapted for schools; these he delivered for some years at different establishments, gaining much approbation, and at length realising sufficient funds to enable him to purchase the business of a Pharmaceutist at Cheshunt in Hertfordshire; this under his management prospered, so that he next determined to qualify as a medical practitioner. He used to start on horseback at 5 o'clock in the morning from Cheshunt for the Charing Cross Hospital, in the medical school of which he became a pupil, returning in the evening in the same way. These journeys were kept up for some years and were of course very fatiguing. In due course my brother obtained the diploma of the Royal College of Surgeons of England and the extra-licence of the Royal College

of Physicians of London. He then started in practice in Richmond, Surrey, where our family had resided for some years and
was well known; after working, almost slaving, for a quarter of a
century and having gained one of the best and most lucrative
practices in the kingdom, he retired, having been able to amass
an ample fortune for his family.'

In actual fact, Richard's obituaries in both the *Lancet* and the
British Medical Journal state he was in practice until a few weeks
before his death.[7]

However, the story is no doubt substantially true, although it
bristles with questions impossible to answer now. Richard
would have finished his apprenticeship to his father by 1832,
but did not take any professional examinations until 1844.
Immediately prior to taking them, he spent eighteen months at
Charing Cross Hospital[8] – so much for 'journeys kept up for
some years.' One assumes that during the ten years 1832–42
he was busy preparing and delivering his lectures. He could not
have delivered them while he was an apprentice, although he
might have had time to read up his subjects. Arthur during his
apprenticeship found ample time to study zoophytes. But why
did Richard not qualify in 1832, for the Hospital could have
been as easily reached from Richmond by horseback as from
Cheshunt; were ten years in the wilderness necessary to gather
fees for eighteen months hospital tuition? The obituaries
quoted also mention he succeeded his father as Surgeon to the
1st Surrey Militia, but not when, perhaps after he started in
practice at Richmond.

It is all very puzzling. Arthur was given his articles by his
uncle, something Richard might have expected since he was the
elder, and he was clearly never short of funds to travel backwards and forwards from Ireland. If Richard had not bought a
chemist's business at Cheshunt Arthur might never have written his *History of the British Freshwater Algae*; the Hertfordshire
streams were a major source of his collection now preserved at
the British Museum. On his own evidence, he got as reasonable
a schooling as was expected by the standards of the time.

He learnt his A B C at 'a small and very primitive day school
in the main street of Teddington kept by an elderly matron
whose name I forget. The instruction was limited to the three
Rs and not much even of these was taught.' Hard cases were

made to stand at the open door with a dunce's cap on their heads in full view of passers-by. One day Arthur stood there thus ornamented, when he spied his father coming down the street. He tore off his cap and bolted indoors, resolved henceforth to lead a blameless life.

A school kept by a Mr Parker at Knapp Hill, Surrey, three miles from Woking, next received him. He was driven over in a cart by a friendly carrier who gave him a lump of blood pudding to keep up his spirits. He devoured it not at first realising what it was made from, 'but I never again regaled myself on blood pudding.'

Mr Parker was 'a worthy and kind-hearted man who had even in those days some loose, but as I dare say some of our sanitary and funeral reformers would teach, correct and advanced notions on the subject of burials. He held the usual mode of interment in little regard, and said he would like to be buried at the foot of an apple tree so as to ensure a good crop of fruit. I do not think his wish was gratified. The pupils consisted of the strong healthy boys and youths of the few tradesmen and farmers of the district and the education was of a restricted character. The surroundings of the house were free and open; the situation cold and bracing, the school room large, with at one end a lofty pulpit, from which prayers were read and a sermon preached on Sundays, as the schoolroom did duty as a chapel for the few inhabitants of the neighbourhood'.

Mr Parker's favourite punishment was a box on the ear that threw the head over to receive a blow on the opposite ear 'until after two or three such blows the recipient was confused, even stunned.' Arthur was fortunate to leave before he was made deaf for life.

His father must have left Teddington about this time, for Arthur was sent next as a day scholar to a school well known at that time on Richmond Green. The headmaster 'whose name I withhold' was a strict disciplinarian. 'He held a high opinion of the virtues of the rod; he was in fact a tyrant and a most unmerciful beater. On one occasion two boys, unable to endure his harshness, ran away, as boys sometimes will, and were not captured for some days; they were placed in a room and fastened by the waist to a heavy weight, were kept thus for at least a day and a night and cruelly beaten at short intervals;

there was much excitement in the school, the master's daughters interceded and at last the punishment came to an end. Were any schoolmaster in these days to attempt anything of the kind, great would be the outcry and severe would be his own punishment but at the time I refer to cruel flogging was commonly practised, even grown-up youths being subjected to the same brutal chastisement; indeed corporal chastisement was considered to be absolutely necessary to the efficient control of the pupils and the maxim thoroughly acted up to, was Spare the rod, spoil the child.'

Happier days dawned when Arthur was removed from this original Salem House Academy* and became a day pupil at a large school kept by a Mr Gibbons, separated only by a paling from his own home in Kew Foot Road. He never saw Mr Gibbons, for he was very ill, and indeed died shortly afterwards. Mrs Gibbons kept the school on, but for young ladies only. The boys school was in charge of a Welshman Mr John George and after Mr Gibbons' death he stayed on in Richmond and received a few pupils, Arthur amongst them, on his own.

Although Mr George was apt to declare, a hand pressed to his side, 'one must have lungs of iron and bones of brass to teach you boys,' Arthur had only the happiest memories of him.

'I have retained throughout life the warmest affection and the most sincere regard for the teacher to whom I was indebted for my love of books and any scholarly knowledge I ever possessed,' and again, 'It was only under the tuition of Mr George that I really began to understand the true object and purpose of education, to experience the pleasure which even the acquisition of scholastic knowledge was capable of giving and to realise the fact, that it was the foundation upon which success or failure in life in many cases mainly rests.'

Mr George unfortunately died 'from a respiratory affection' at a comparatively early age, too soon to witness the triumph of his influence in Arthur's steady progress in life.

The house at Kew Foot Road had a nice old garden with a brick wall at one side on which peach, plum, nectarine and greengage trees 'were trained while apple and pear trees were scattered over the ground. In this my brother Richard and I

* To which David Copperfield was banished.

used to work, digging, wheeling, weeding under the direction of an old soldier who had fought at Waterloo and was a great favourite with my father and indeed with us all.'

He further undertook care of the little garden plots of the pupils next door and often rose at six a.m. to attend to them before the day's lessons began.

There was a large garden, too, at the next Richmond home in the Vineyard. 'I took to rearing orange, lemon and tamarind trees from the pips and stones and was very proud of my success. I formed a little hot or forcing bed with the grass mown from the lawn, and used to take our visitors to see my orange plants, now and again bestowing one on any favourite friend or visitor.'

Quite early on, therefore, Arthur acquired that taste for botany that led to his *History of the Algae*, researches at Kew and the offer of a Lectureship in Botany; and incidentally, reading about it all gives no impression of 'very narrow resources' and 'shortage of funds.'

While he busied himself in these innocent pursuits, cholera crept closer across Europe, fostered in the hot-bed of stinking city slums. The *little cloud of pestilence* first discerned far away over India in 1818 now filled the sky and its hideous shadow fell across England. Navy patrols directed ships from suspect ports into official quarantine stations, but none the less the disease appeared at Sunderland in 1831, probably introduced by a German sailor.

The first officially recognised case was diagnosed one Sunday afternoon in October 1831.[9] From Sunderland it flared rapidly north into Scotland and south into England.

Arthur probably listened to the prayer circulated that November to be read out in churches: 'Oh merciful Father, suffer not Thy destroying angel to lift up his hand against us.' It proved unavailing, and cholera appeared in London the following year and was responsible for 11,000 cases with 5,275 deaths, and Arthur heard for the first time of the mysterious and terrifying disease that was to tax his skill and courage to the utmost during the third epidemic of 1853 and with which Richard, too, had to grapple.

He wrote a pamphlet on the subject[10] in which he states that Richmond suffered in 1832 as well as in 1849, but Arthur makes no mention in his autobiography of this first outbreak. We are thus left ignorant whether his father had cases and what he thought of its appearance at Sunderland where his father practised. Very probably he knew Dr Reid Clanny, chosen by the local Board of Health at Sunderland to head a special committee of doctors which may have included Hassall senior.

Arthur's boyhood closed with the gift of his indentures from his uncle Sir James Murray, M.D. (Dublin), who had married his mother's sister. 'This generous offer relieved my father of a great deal of anxiety and much expense on my account.'

Sir James had a fashionable practice in Dublin and offered 'to take me into his house.' Accordingly, Arthur sailed for Ireland from the Thames in the autumn of 1834 aboard the steam packet *Shannon*, 180 feet, 513 tons, engines of 160 h.p.[11] She called at Portsmouth and Falmouth, and the journey took five or six days. It was one with which Arthur was to become familiar. As E. G. Clayton[12] pointed out in 1909, 'to sail from the Liffey to the Thames took longer than does now a passage to New York.'

References for Chapter One

All extracts in this and succeeding chapters unless otherwise stated are taken from *The Narrative of a Busy Life* by Arthur Hill Hassall, Longmans 1893.

1 *History through Surnames*, W. O. Hassall, Pergamon Press 1967.
2, 7 *British Medical Journal*, 1 Jan. 1876, and *Lancet* 22 Jan. 1876.
3 J. Keith Bishop, County Archivist, Durham County Council.
4 John H. Rumsby, Durham Light Infantry Museum, Aykley Heads, Durham.
5 *Faithful; the Story of the Durham Light Infantry*, S. P. G. Ward, Thomas Nelson (no date, Foreword 1962).
6 *Irish Battles*, G. A. Hayes McCoy, Longmans 1969.
8 G. H. Cooper, Keeper of Manuscripts, Guildhall Library, London.
9 *Alive and Well*, Norman Longmate, Penguin Books 1970.
10 *Cholera: Its Nature and Treatment*, Richard Hassall, MD, Henry Renshaw, London 1854.
11 *British Paddle Steamers*, Geoffrey Body, David and Charles 1971.
12 *A Compendium of Food Microscopy*, E. G. Clayton, Baillière Tindall & Cox 1909.

Notes to the text of Chapter One

Teddington Parish Church. I am most grateful to the Reverend Thomas C. Elsam, St Alban's Vicarage, Teddington, for information about the former parish church at Teddington, the correct spelling of Mrs Hassall's Christian name and her place of burial, and for furnishing a copy of Arthur's baptismal certificate.

John Coppin Esq: The following extracts from Venn: *Alumni Cantabrigienses* and the *Trinity Admissions Register* were kindly supplied by Mrs Alison Sproston, Assistant Librarian, Trinity College Library, Cambridge.

COPPIN John Adm. pens. (age 18) at Trinity, May 24, 1839. S. of John B. Jan 15, 1821, at Tynemouth, Northumberland, School Richmond, Yorks (Mr Tate). Matric. Michs. 1839; B.A. 1843; M.A. 1846. Adm. at Lincolns Inn, Jan. 26, 1842, as s'of John, late of North Shields, deceased. Called to the Bar, 1846. Of Bingfield Corbridge-on-Tyne. Purchased the estate known as Bingfield East Side, 1876, and resided there. Died Nov. 1st, 1891, aged 70. Buried at Halston. (Foster; *Men at the Bar History of Northumberland* IV 234.)

Coppin John. Born at Tynemouth, Northumberland. School, Richmond, Yorkshire (Mr Tate.) Age 18. Pensioner May 24, 1839. Tutor, Prof. Whewell. (Matriculated 1839; B.A. 1843; M.A. 1846.)

The *Burial of Thomas Hassall*
Arthur tells us that when he went to Addison Road in 1842 'my father and my sister Eliza accompanied me.' (He does not mention Ann, who presumably remained at Cheshunt until Richard wound up his business there in 1843.) He and his father and Eliza would no doubt attend St Barnabas in Addison Road, just as the Hassall family had attended St Mary's at Teddington. In those days a local practitioner, especially a young one like Arthur, just starting practice in the neighbourhood, was expected to attend the local church regularly.

St Barnabas was built in 1827 but the Vicar, the Rev. P. P. Kirwin, M.A., has kindly explained that although there were burials in the crypt, as shown by a number of memorials in the church, there is no record of them except for a short period 1849–1853. Until St Barnabas became a separate parish in 1853, earlier records were held by the parent parish of St Mary's Abbots, and thanks are expressed to the Vicar, H. L. O. Rees, M.A., Rural Dean of Kensington, and the Verger, D. Light Esq., for a search of the burial register between 1842 – 1844. No entry of Thomas Hassall was however found.

TWO

Anatomy and Leeches

Writing at the close of the nineteenth century when an increasing number of doctors were appearing who possessed a joint qualification both in surgery and 'physic' or medicine, Arthur found it advisable to explain in his autobiography published in 1893 that in England the medical profession is divided into two branches, the surgical and the medical. *For each of these a somewhat different course of study and two separate diplomas were formerly required.**

The system existing when he was a student is illustrated by three memorials that make the old church of St Mary the Virgin in Cauldwell Street, Bedford, more interesting than its Norman tower. Other churches too have Norman towers, some even boast a Saxon one, but I know of no other church possessing three tablets to doctors that span two hundred years of medical history. John Beaumont, born 1616, Henry Fleming, died 1774 and William Campion, who died in 1810, all practised in the town. But whereas John and Henry were physicians, William was a surgeon.

A physician was a university graduate in medicine or a Member of the Royal College of Physicians of London. A surgeon was not a university graduate, he held a diploma, not a degree; he was M.R.C.S., Member of the Royal College of Surgeons of England (originally of London) or of an equivalent body in Scotland or Ireland.

A physician prescribed 'physic', medicine, but did not dispense it. This was the jealously guarded prerogative of the apothecary, who was a member of the old Apothecaries Company better known as the Society of Apothecaries. Nor was a surgeon permitted to dispense it (although an apothecary could practise surgery).[1] Arthur therefore had to obtain the diploma

* Present writer's italics.

of the Society after he became M.R.C.S., thus acquiring the two diplomas he mentions. Two years before he was born, in 1815, the Apothecaries Act had been passed requiring students who intended to become apothecaries in England and Wales to serve an apprenticeship of five years to a general practitioner before spending about a year at one of the great hospitals. Samuel Fothergill, writing in 1812, pointed out that so many apothecaries were now practising surgery, medicine and obstetrics in addition to their own proper trade of pharmacy that in future they should be referred to as General Practitioners, perhaps the first time the expression was used.[2]

Arthur embarked on practice in Notting Hill in 1842 on the strength of his two diplomas as Mr Hassall, Surgeon. He met no formal difficulties when he subsequently took the M.D. of London University, or University College as it then was, although in the eighteenth century William Hunter was fined by the Surgeons Company for leaving them to practise as a physician. Originally a surgeon who wished to become a physician had to go through a tedious business of disenfranchisement and sever himself completely from his former profession before he was permitted to practise the new.

The qualifications of his father have not been traced. There is no mention of him in the lists of the College of Surgeons (or of the earlier Surgeons Company) nor in the records of the Barber-Surgeons Company between 1757 and 1817. A Thomas Hassal, with one l, however appears as a Yeoman of the Society of Apothecaries in the Medical Registers of 1780 and 1783. The term described anyone who was free of the Society but had not yet been promoted liveryman; in practical terms it usually seems to have implied an apothecary who was qualified but had not yet set himself up in independent practice.[3]

This particular Hassal was made free by redemption (i.e. by purchase) on 16 May 1766 after serving an apprenticeship of seven years to a Mr Thomas Dawes, apothecary in Coventry. He must have been in his twenties then, and supposing he was born in or about 1745, is not likely to have been the father of a son born in 1817.

Yet our Thomas not only puts himself down as Surgeon on Arthur's baptismal certificate, but is described as Surgeon and Apothecary in the registration of Richard's apprenticeship in

the Entry Qualification Books of the Society of Apothecaries.
One would expect that the Society were satisfied that he was
what he claimed to be, in particular that he was indeed an
apothecary although of course if he was a Yeoman of the Society
or had been one, no questions would be raised.

Arthur confuses the problem by mentioning that one of the
examiners for his M.R.C.S. was a Mr Anthony White; 'he was a
friend of my father and I was myself acquainted with him.'
Would an examiner of the College be on friendly terms with a
self-styled Surgeon who had never presented himself for the
College examinations? Or come to that, for those of the Apothecaries Society, unless he was a former Yeoman of the Company?

If Arthur is mistaken and his father was 83, not 73, when he
died, then he was born about 1762; twenty-one when the 1783
Register was published but only eighteen when that of 1780
appeared. (And thirty-six, nearly twenty years older than she,
when he met Miss Ann Sherrock aged eighteen.)

This is assuming that the given year of purchase is incorrect;
mistakes may occur, for the Society's candidate qualification
books state that Arthur was born in 1816, not 1817 as recorded
on his baptismal certificate.

He appears too late in the records to be Arthur's grandfather,
the surgeon practising at Sunderland, and the only other
possibility is that Thomas Hassall, Arthur's father, went north
after finishing his apprenticeship and acquired a diploma from
a Scottish school, although his name does not appear in the list
of Edinburgh medical graduates from 1705 to 1866.[4]

It was quite feasible in those days to practise medicine
without any formal qualifications. There were quite a number
of unqualified assistants to be found when Arthur died at the
close of the century. Thomas Hassall however would scarcely
be a friend of an examiner for the College of Surgeons if he had
not taken some formal qualification after completing an apprenticeship to his father or some other unknown practitioner.

Surgery, even minor surgery, was a hazardous business in
those pre-antiseptic days not only for the patient but the
surgeon, too. It is to be remarked that the surgeon recorded in
St Mary's lived only half as long as the two physicians. John
Beaumont lived to be eighty and Henry Fleming to be eighty-
five, but William Campion was only forty-four when he died.

John and Henry were the physicians who seldom touched a patient except possibly to take a pulse, who sat and listened to his tale of woe before giving an opinion. It was the surgeon's calling that brought him into close physical contact with patients often unwashed and frequently verminous, and he who was hourly exposed to the risk of fatal blood-poisoning from the prick of an infected needle or the scratch of a broken bone. Hospitals of course were stinking charnel houses in whose wards there was not only a metaphorical fog but an almost visible miasma from putrefying wounds.

As late as 1866 Christopher Heath, F.R.C.S., warns readers of his handbook *Minor Surgery and Bandaging for the use of House Surgeons and Junior Practitioners* that unless due precautions are taken 'the foul air of a hospital produces an effect upon the strongest constitution within a few weeks.' This was the background to the new life now opening out before Arthur.

'Arrived in Merrion Square,' he writes, 'I was most kindly received by my uncle and aunt; soon occupation was found for me and I quickly became aware that the business of my life, with for me its great events and issues, had commenced in earnest.

'My uncle, Sir James Murray, was an energetic, self-reliant, thoughtful and indeed clever man; his earlier years were passed in Belfast where as a chemist he flourished and made a fortune. Eventually he removed to Dublin and when I arrived he was living in Merrion Square, practising as a physician. He was physician to the then Lord Lieutenant of Ireland, the Marquis of Anglesea, who was a martyr to neuralgia. Sir James was able to afford him considerable relief and received at his hands the honour of knighthood. My uncle was the author, amongst other publications, of an original work on the use of compressed and rarified air, applied by means of certain ingenious mechanical arrangements to the surface of the body for the treatment of various morbid conditions and symptoms. There can be no doubt of the value of some of the suggestions made therein, although the book is itself now forgotten and the methods described in it but rarely put into practice.

'Sir James being a good practical chemist perceived at a very early period the objections to be urged against the administration of the but little soluble preparations of magnesia and he succeeded in making an agreeable effervescent solution. He was the first to devise this preparation, which has now for a great many years been known as Murray's Magnesia. The solution, possessing many advantages, was and still is in considerable demand and it has yielded for a long period a handsome revenue.'

For all he says to the contrary, Arthur was the only apprentice of his uncle. This may have been so, but is unlikely. Sir James had substantial means and would not rely on student's fees as a source of income, but his eminence would attract pupils. Dr George Johnston of zoophyte fame with whom Arthur later corresponded was one of seven apprentices when he was articled to Dr James Abercrombie in 1813, and Arthur mentions a cousin Mr John Murray – a son of Sir James? – 'who was author of some political novels and of a pamphlet bearing the striking title *The Court Doctor dissected*, having reference to the sad case of Lady Flora Hastings.' Harley Williams states that the author of this 'venomous brochure' was an unknown doctor.[5] John Murray therefore qualified in medicine, and since the tragedy of Lady Flora occurred within two or three years of the accession of Queen Victoria in 1837, he was very probably a fellow student with Arthur, and if there was one, there may have been others, although Arthur mentions none.

It was Arthur however who was singled out by his uncle shortly after his arrival for a particularly invidious task, possibly as a hint he must not expect preferential treatment.

Apart from his practice, 'Sir James was Inspector of Anatomy for Dublin. In that city all persons who died in public hospitals, infirmaries and the like, if not claimed within forty-eight hours, were delivered to the different medical schools for dissection.'

The Anatomy Act of 1832 had authorised the use of unclaimed bodies by specially licensed schools. Removal and distribution of the bodies was carried out by the Inspector's staff 'and after a time,' writes Arthur, 'some of these duties were entrusted to me. I had to see that distribution of the subjects was impartially and discreetly carried out.' Bearing in mind the difficulties and slowness of travel at that time, the wisdom of a Solomon must have been invoked to deal with 'difficulties and unpleasantness that arose from relatives turning up and claiming bodies after the expiration of the statutory limit.' One sympathises with the startled lecturer at a Canadian school of anatomy when one of the students demanded, 'What for you got mon oncle here?' although on learning mon oncle could be released to him for burial at his own expense, he replied, 'Suppose mon oncle come, suppose mon oncle stay.'

It must have been a soul-searching experience for the school-boy hitherto engaged in the harmless pursuit of raising orange trees from pips.

'These inspections in the early days of my medical career were by no means pleasant, and I naturally shrank from the awful sights of poor dead humanity, emaciated and disfigured by disease and made still more hideous by the anatomist's scalpel . . . Madame Tussaud's Chamber of Horrors is less trying to view than a large dissecting room with several bodies more or less decomposed. . . .'

Subjects would not be in mint condition forty-eight hours after death and in the absence of formalin or other adequate preservatives classes in anatomy for obvious reasons were held in the winter.

'The chief of the men employed to convey the unclaimed bodies to the schools was a man named Bowman, a remarkably civil and obliging fellow, fond though he was of a drop of the *cratur*. It appeared he had a dread that some day or other he might himself be extended full length upon one of the usual tables; this fear, I afterwards learnt, was not unfounded as his body was actually conveyed to one of the schools; some of the pupils recognising the man and knowing of this dread, clubbed together and had him decently buried.'

Arthur continues: 'My uncle gave me some introductory works to read as preparation for the lectures which were to follow. The first course of lectures I attended was delivered in the medical session of 1834–35 and this was followed by other courses in the four following winters, and in one or two summer sessions, but usually I returned to England in the summer.'

Travelling backwards and forwards on the *Shannon* Arthur says that 'being a good sailor I enjoyed these trips immensely. The last I heard of the *Shannon* was that she had been totally wrecked on one of her journeys. On one occasion I remember I went to Liverpool with my cousin Mr John Murray on the outside of the Tally Ho! coach; the journey extended over 24 hours, that is, a day and a night; the cold at night was intense and I thought I should have died; as it was my cousin was laid up in Liverpool with pneumonia brought on by the exposure. Such occurrences in the coaching days must have been common.' Arthur was fortunate to suffer no worse ill effects. In later years he developed phythisis, and Keats' fatal consumption was precipitated by getting chilled through on the outside of a coach travelling the short distance from London to Hampstead.

The schools Arthur attended were chiefly those of Peters Street, Digges Street and Trinity College, and the hospitals, the Jervis Street and Mercers Hospitals and the Netterville Dispensary his uncle had founded and which had only a small number of beds.

'At the period to which I refer the Dublin School of Medicine, ranking always high, stood at its highest; there was a crowd of able men in the profession, including both teachers and practitioners. Amongst the former may be mentioned Harrison, Apjohn, Hilles, Hayden, Ellis, Ireland and Bellingham; while among those who were devoted more particularly to medical and surgical practice, Colles, Stokes, Carmichael, Graves, Crampton, Corrigan, Marsh may be enumerated. Some of these were world-renowned men, and even in these days they are well-remembered names and high authorities on the subjects to which their talents were specially devoted.'

Robert James Graves (1796–1853) and his contemporary William Stokes (1804–78) 'rank among the greatest physicians of their time. They were the leaders of the Irish school.'[6] They are remembered today whenever Graves disease or Cheyne-Stokes breathing are in question. Benjamin Colles (1773–1843), the great surgeon of the Dublin school, is still recalled by Colles fracture and Colles Law. Nor will the name of Dominic (later Sir Dominic) John Corrigan be forgotten so long as a 'water-hammer' pulse is encountered. He attended Arthur when serious illness interrupted his studies, and he was the first to describe fibroid phthisis not occurring in miners, the disease that overtook Arthur early in middle life and finally drove him out of London.

'Sir James Murray,' writes Arthur, 'from his influential position was enabled to obtain for me free admissions to the

whole of the requisite courses of lectures and to the
All this education being free in addition to the
indentures. Well might Arthur declare in after ye
therefore rested under the deepest obligations to my uncle ion
this, as well as on other accounts.'

There can be no doubt that he appreciated it all and worked
hard to make the very most of his opportunities. 'I was more
than diligent, made fair progress and gained some prizes,
including one for Botany of which throughout life I have always
been fond.' He would enjoy those botanical excursions described by Albert Smith, the surgeon-dentist author of *The
Adventures of Christopher Tadpole* (1848) and other tales, 'as
belonging to the most insane department of a medical man's
education.' Of course, Arthur was an old hand at the subject,
but Mr Barnes the medical student, one of Albert Smith's
characters, although in most other respects a very old hand
indeed, 'his ideas of botany had always been connected with
visions of pretty girls holding small green water pots painted
red inside but he found it quite different when he began to study
it in earnest.' As Albert Smith puts it, 'These trips are insisted
upon at the schools. The lecturers keep up the interest by
proposing enterprising botanical excursions every week during
the session, when the students generally consume an immense
quantity of cheese and biscuits, drink a great deal of half-and-
half, collect a few wild weeds from the hedges in tin candle
boxes and come home—not exactly tipsy, but as Mr Barnes
remarked "All nohow, like a wasp in a whirlwind"—in any
inbound omnibus, if they have sixpence left to pay the fare.'[7]

'For medical degrees or licenses a candidate had to attend a
course of lectures delivered in a botanic garden registered for
the purpose.'[8] Furthermore, 'In the first quarter of the
nineteenth century botany, in the universities, was regarded as
a study "ancillary to that of *Materia Medica*" and as a means of
enabling the practitioners to recognise the plants used in
medicine when there might be no druggist to appeal to.'[8] Good
reason, therefore, why Arthur mentions his attendance at
Trinity College, to follow the course given by William Allman,
M.D., Professor of Botany.* The Botanical Garden was the

* Elected 16 January 1809 and superannuated 4 March 1844.

famous one at Balls Bridge, 'which still remains such a useful
and ornamental adjunct to the University.'[9] The regulations of
the Board stipulated that the Professor lectured four times a
week from 15 April to 15 July, 'provided that if he chooses to
conduct his pupils into the country in order to examine the
native plants once a week his doing so shall be considered as
equivalent to a lecture.' All students of the University might
attend the first twelve lectures free, and the remainder were
confined to those who paid fees. The fee was raised to £1.10.0 on
13 July 1811.

Arthur would have attended every lecture assiduously but
his uncle's eminence would have ensured he was put to no
expense. The thorough grounding he absorbed on his favourite
subject proved invaluable in the future.

According to one's point of view it might be 'the insane
department of a medical education' but at least it got students
out of the reeking wards and dissecting rooms into the fresh
air. Arthur's tutors were certainly quite as well aware as
Christopher Heath previously quoted of the baleful influence of
hospital air, and it provided exercise, too; as Heath remarks, 'a
daily walk is the great means for maintaining the health and
spirits; the walk, particularly, is essential, and is very apt to be
shirked, either from want of energy or over-anxiety for the
welfare of cases.'

In 1837 Arthur secured his first medical qualification, a
diploma in Midwifery. 'At a very early period of my studies, I
was required to attend lectures on Midwifery and the Diseases
of Women and afterwards to attend cases at the Anglesea
Lying-In Hospital.

'Certain students were told off in turn to be on duty at this
Hospital, some by day, others at night, they also being liable to
be called to confinements within a certain radius round the
Hospital. Of these duties I had my share, young as I was,
indeed so youthful was I in both appearance and reality, that I
was called "the boy doctor", whose services nevertheless were
in frequent request.

'I could relate some curious experiences during my attendance at this Hospital; the district surrounding it was extremely
poor and wretched and some of the patients to whom I was
summoned were in the most abject poverty. I have seen them in

the hour of their need lying on straw on the floor, in a room without furniture, without food, not even the ordinary gruel, fire or light. Under such circumstances the first thing to be done was to provide these requisites. Often the rooms were inconveniently crowded with numbers of sympathetic friends, as well as occasionally a drunken husband, who had to be turned out; an operation not always easy to accomplish.

'I remember well one frosty night in mid-winter being called out to attend a poor woman who was suddenly taken ill in the street. I found her lying in the middle of the bare, frost-bound and sparkling road, with no other attendant than an old watchman with his dull and dismal lamp. The woman and her infant were conveyed to the Hospital, where the mother made quite as good a recovery and the child thrived as well as if they had been born to the purple and surrounded by every comfort and luxury. The above incident occurred shortly before the inauguration of the new Police, or Peelers, between whom on their first appearance and the medical students, a fierce war was carried on for some time with snow balls flying in every direction.'

He left Merrion Square for a 'well-known first-class boarding house in Harcourt Street,' and from there went to 'a sparsely-furnished bedroom on the third floor of a house in Digges Street, where for such slight attendance as was needed I was waited on by a red-legged and bare-footed peasant girl. I now diligently devoted myself to my studies; most of my reading was done in the early mornings and evenings. I used to get up at five and six o'clock in the dark wintry mornings and read by the aid of a rushlight, and my breakfast consisted of a sugarless decoction of cocoa nibs and dry butterless bread; the other meals not being on a very liberal scale.'

The changes were necessary, he explains, in order to be close to his work, no doubt true enough since he attended the Digges Street School; possibly at the back of his mind was the thought he could not be reached so easily there to act as *ad hoc* Inspector of Anatomy.

Observing that 'I took a very cheap and humble apartment, being now entirely on my own resources. These were very limited and I was anxious to save expense as far as possible,' he adds. 'It was not so much that funds were deficient as that any small sum I could save out of my allowance was spent on books or on an occasional treat to the gallery or pit of the theatre, sometimes accompanied by my cousin, Edward Murray. At the time, the great attraction was that inimitable master of melo-drama, Power, who it will be remembered was lost years ago on his way to New York, when every soul on board the vessel perished, not one being left to tell the tale of this great catas-trophe.' Was cousin Edward Murray a fellow pupil under Sir James?

However excellent were the reasons that prompted the move to Digges Street, the result was disastrous. It was a pity he ever left Merrion Square, where his aunt would have been anxious to look after her deceased sister's youngest boy and he would at least have been fed on something rather more sustaining than cocoa nibs and dry bread. To quote Christopher Heath once more, he advocates good meals as a most important safeguard against the poisonous influence of hospital air.

'What with hard study, poor food and insanitary surround-ings,' Arthur writes, 'after a while I fell ill. For a time I struggled against the illness, but one day, when more from habit than anything else, I had made my way to the dissecting room and not being able to work, perched myself on one of the high stools usually found in similar places, I became speedily worse and was compelled to go to my room and to bed; before leaving the dissecting room I gave one of my fellow English students some money to buy leeches and I asked him to apply them to my temples . . . before they were detached I became insensible.'

When he recovered his senses, his uncle was at his bedside.

'The remedy,' Arthur writes, 'the leeches, was one which in these days would not be generally approved for a severe case of typhoid fever.' He was writing sixty years later, when memory of his symptoms must have been confused with those of later illness, and with knowledge not available when he was a student. It is possible he was struck down by typhus, not typhoid. The two infections were not clearly distinguished until 1850 by Sir William Jenner, barely in time to identify the fatal illness of the Prince Consort. Typhus was rife among the poor of great cities, and those Arthur Hassall attended at the Anglesea Hospital or anywhere else were the very poor who had nowhere else to go and for whom the hospitals were provided. They were filthy, lousy and verminous, but to Arthur it was all in the day's work if he was bitten by their fleas or brushed their lice off his coat cuffs, happily ignorant that typhus is transmitted by the bite of infected body lice.

Typhoid contracted in the primitive conditions of Digges Street, squalid by modern sanitary standards, or typhus innocently bequeathed to the 'boy doctor' by the woman in labour he attended, so far as Sir James was concerned his nephew had a fever, 'slow nervous' or 'putrid' if one wished to be pedantic, but still fever, for which the popular treatment was a low diet and bleeding by leeches.

In 1833, when Broussais, the great French advocate of the treatment, was at the height of his fame, 14,000,000 leeches were imported into France.[6]

'Sir James, with occasionally, Dr, afterwards Sir Dominic, Corrigan, attended me throughout a very long and dangerous illness,' Arthur writes, 'during part of which I was delirious.' They would be aware that their illustrious contemporary Robert Graves considered that his chief claim to fame might be that he fed fevers, and since it was obvious Arthur had been on starvation rations, they may have spared him the low regimen if not the leeches. Be that as it may, 'the united skill and care of these physicians brought me through the crisis and after some weeks, I had so far recovered, as to be able to be removed into the country.' He remarks that it was fortunate his illness fell on him towards the end of the winter session, so that it was not lost time but counted in his curriculum of studies; however, it was a disappointment as he had hoped to go in for some prizes, chiefly of books. 'There were no great pecuniary rewards in those days, such as are now given in most medical schools and colleges, to stimulate study and help the impecunious but diligent student on his uphill way; however the disappointment was in a subsequent session made up by the prize for Botany being awarded me.'

For his convalescence, he tells us, he was transferred to a 'scrupulously clean bright apartment at Monkstown ... through the agency of friends, Mr and Mrs Alder, to whom I became everlastingly indebted for kindnesses innumerable, continued over a long series of years. I can only give but feeble

34   BY CANDLELIGHT

expression to the feelings I experienced on the journey into the country from the darkness of Digges Street; it was like a resurrection.'

References for Chapter Two

1 *Lancet*, 1.112. 1830
2 *The Healers*, Kurt Pollak, M.D., in collaboration with E. Ashworth Underwood, F.R.C.P., Nelson 1968.
3 C. R. H. Cooper, Keeper of Manuscripts, Guildhall Library, London.
4 Joan Emmerson, Assistant Librarian, University of Newcastle upon Tyne.
5 *The Healing Touch*, Harley Williams, Jonathan Cape 1949.
6 *A Short History of Medicine*, Charles Singer & E. Ashworth Underwood, 2nd edit., Oxford University Press 1962.
7 Albert Richard Smith, author of *The Adventures of Christopher Tadpole* (1848), *The Adventures of Mr Ledbury* (1851) etc. These works in particular shed a delightful light on the medical students of that time.
8 *Joseph Dalton Hooker*, W. B. Turrill.
9 *History of the Medical Teaching in Trinity College Dublin and the School of Physic in Ireland*, T. P. C. Kirkpatrick, Dublin 1912.

THREE
Excursions into Zoology

'I lately,' writes Arthur, 'had an opportunity of beholding this novel and interesting sight of the phosphorescence of zoophytes to great advantage, when on board one of the Devonshire trawling boats that frequent this coast. The trawl was raised at midnight, and great quantities of corallines were entangled in the meshes of the network, all shining like myriads of the brightest diamonds.'[1]

While at Dublin he made an extensive study of Irish zoophytes, 'those productions which, bearing a strong resemblance to vegetables, in form and some other particulars, are yet of an animal nature.'[1] (Sea-anemones and corals are examples.*)

His interest in these creatures may possibly be attributed to his meeting the Northumbrian naturalist Joshua Alder on a visit to his own relatives at Newcastle on Tyne. Joshua was born in Newcastle in 1792 and died there on 21 June 1867; his great work on *Nudibranchiata Mollusca* was published by the Ray Society. One of the founders of the Natural History Society of Newcastle in 1829 and of the Tyneside Naturalists Field Club in 1849, he produced catalogues of the mollusca and also the zoophytes of Northumberland and Durham for the Tyneside Naturalists Club. Dr George Johnston, the zoophyte authority of that day, expresses thanks to him and also a Mr Bowman, also of Newcastle, in the first edition of his *British Zoophytes* (1838), and again in the preface of the second edition (1847). Arthur may have met Joshua at a meeting of the Newcastle Natural History Society. It would be difficult to establish a connection between Joshua and his friends the Dublin Alders, but such a relationship is not impossible especially as the Alders were a trading family specialising in food imports.[3]

* Zoophytes, plant-animals, are classified today among the Coelenterates and Polyzoa.

They may safely be assumed to have had Newcastle connec-
tions, and it would be natural for Arthur to look them up,
perhaps armed with introductions.

He would be further encouraged in his field studies to learn
that an apothecary in Naples called Ferrante Imperato was
apparently the first to declare the animality of corals and
madrepores in his *Historia Naturae* printed at Naples in 1599 and
reprinted in 1627. He mentions the fact, quoting Dr Johnston as
authority, in one of seven papers he contributed to the *Annals of
Natural History* 1841–2–3. This particular paper[2] is illustrated
'by beautiful drawings for which I am indebted to the skill and
perseverance of a lady whose name I would willingly mention
were I authorised to do so.' In his autobiography he reveals that
the artist was Miss Hunter, a sister of Mrs Alder.

'In time I made a considerable collection of Irish zoophytes,
many of these being new to the British and Irish fauna; while
others had not before been observed, although described in
some foreign works . . . I was not content to limit my searches to
the sea shore, so in the hope of obtaining some rare and new
species, I used to go into the sea itself; for this purpose I
provided myself with a special costume, this allowed of my
turning over the loose pieces of rock which were under the water
but still near the shore and which had in great abundance been
placed there as a barrier against the encroachments of the sea;
this proceeding yielded a rich reward.'

In order to pursue his quarry into deep waters, he made the
trip mentioned in the opening quotation; forty years later the
experience had been so sharply etched upon his memory he
recalled it as vividly as if it had happened yesterday.

'Encouraged by the results just recorded, I next determined
that I would see what was to be obtained from the deep sea
itself. At the period to which I allude the chief fishing and
trawling on the Irish coast were in the hands of a number of
fishermen or trawlers from Devonshire; these men had good
boats, they were steady and experienced and mostly teetotal-
lers. I therefore arranged to accompany them on one of their
trawling expeditions. The crew consisted of three men, all
strangers to me.

'We started from Kingstown Harbour one bitterly cold
afternoon in November; a fresh breeze was blowing and the

boat pitched about so much that I found it necessary to sit down and catch fast hold of the taffrail to prevent myself, as it seemed to me, from being thrown bodily into the sea. I had not been in this position very long before I heard the crash of broken bottles; this was occasioned by an accident to a hamper of good things in the way of food and drink I had brought with me and which had been abundantly provided by my ever kind friends the Alders, with whom I was staying at the time. We started somewhat late in the afternoon, so that it was soon night; the boat was strongly built, with a large deck and a cabin and four berths; but these were filled with different kinds of gear and tackle and it was obvious that they were never used; one of the berths was cleared out for me; it was very dirty and had only a thin hard mattress, however I soon turned in, but at first not to sleep; the surroundings and situation were so new and strange and then the incessant tramping of the men in their heavy boots, the clanking of chains, the noise of the sea and wind effectually prevented sleep that first night.

'Somewhat late, two of the men descended from the deck and at once lay down, fully extended on the bare boards at the bottom of the cabin in their immense jack boots and tarpaulin hats and soon they were fast asleep, as was plainly manifested by their loud snoring which was even more disturbing than the noise of the sea; they were not allowed to sleep very long at a time as the calls to duty in the night were pretty frequent. Of course at first I deplored the loss of my hamper but afterwards not at all; although I am an exceptionally good sailor I found I had little appetite for ordinary food and still less for stimulants. The crew of the trawler lived principally on fish, chiefly soles and plaice, baked before the fire and on soup made with a little meat or fish, mixed vegetables and abundance of salt. I found this kind of food so nice and appetising that I partook of the same meals as the fishermen; the contents of the hamper were not wholly lost and some meat, fowls and whiskey remained; these I offered the men, but the whiskey they would not touch. We used to travel backwards and forwards some miles from the shore along the Mourne Mountains between Kingstown and Belfast, making several trips during the week.

'The trawl or net is heavily weighted and sinks readily . . . it is usually down some six or eight hours, being dragged along by the boat with its sails set; it is raised by means of the capstan and windlass, the labour of this being somewhat hard and the time required considerable; I noticed particularly that very few seaweeds were brought up by the trawl but chiefly corallines, the very things I was in search of; the comparative absence of seaweeds is explained by the fact that they require more light than is to be found at the depth at which the trawling is carried on . . . The raising of the trawl and opening of the net even in the daytime is always interesting and instructive, but at night, the sight is brilliant and beautiful in the extreme. As the trawl nears the surface and is swayed to and fro by the waves and the motion of the boat, great flashes of phosphorescent fire and light are evoked . . . Another beautiful phenomenon was that of the phosphorescence of the sea itself . . . the sea fell from the boat in never ceasing drops, flashes and wavelets of colour, bright and varied as that emitted by the diamond, while from the rudder a long stream of phosphorescent light followed in the wake of the vessel; the sea seemed all aglow, as if on fire.' He adds, 'Although this phenomenon was not produced by corallines, as in the case previously described, it was yet due to a similar cause; namely the presence in the water of minute gelatinous organisms, which when the water was agitated freely gave forth their living fire.'

Finally, 'Having been at sea for about a week in the coldest and roughest weather of the month of November we returned to Kingstown, I laden with a goodly assortment of the treasures of the deep. I shook hands, most cordially and not without regret, with my hardy, adventurous and kind companions. When we started they were entirely unknown to me or my friends. I neither knew their names or characters or even the name of their boat,' and he adds, no doubt with the tragic loss at sea of his eldest brother in mind, 'it occurred to me afterwards that under other circumstances the trip might not have been free from danger. I might have been tossed overboard in the dead of night and there would have been no one to tell the tale.'

He corresponded with Dr George Johnston, 'the great authority at that time on the subject,' and quotes with pride a paragraph from another work of Johnston's, *British Sponges* (1842), where he remarks that 'Mr Arthur Hill Hassall, whom I claim as my pupil in zoophytology and likely ere long to surpass his master therein, also sent me several sponges from Dublin Bay and other localities.' Among the new or rare species that Arthur secured that form living encrustations upon any suitable surface Johnston named one after him *Lepralia Hassallii*. Another zoophyte was called *Coryne Hassallii* by Professor Edward Forbes after Arthur had shown it was responsible for spinous encrustations on shells thrown up on the shore, a fact that the Professor had at first disputed.

Arthur extended his researches by occasional visits to Cullercoats near Tynemouth on visits to relatives at North Shields; as mentioned previously, 'the family consisted of my cousin Mrs Coppin who was a Miss Hassall, her son and my life-long friend Mr John Coppin, and my aunt, Mrs Sanderson, a sister of my father.' Among specimens that John Coppin submitted, Arthur writes, 'I recognised two new species, one of which ranked as a new genus and I named it Coppinia, a genus which has been accepted by subsequent writers.'

All trace is now lost, alas, of the collection of Irish zoophytes and shells from 'the splendid sands of Clontarf' which he gathered and presented to the Dublin Natural History Society 'where they were preserved for many years'.[4] However, it is still possible to consult the list of the Invertebrata found in Dublin Bay and its vicinity published with his other reports in the *Annals of Natural History*. These grow more priceless with the years as records of the species and genera found in the district a hundred and thirty years ago.

Arthur's field studies were inevitably accompanied by adventures, hazards familiar to those who engage in such work. 'Passing round Bray Head one evening I had to take to the water and with considerable difficulty clamber over some awkward boulders and rocks.' On another occasion he was almost trapped by the tide while working on the Boars Back, a ridge of rocks near Cullercoats. 'I heard cries and shouts . . . sooner they grew louder, denoting alarm . . . I looked up and saw to my dismay I was surrounded by water . . . I could not swim. I finally reached the shore half-drowned . . . taking care not to land in the middle of the crowd as I was rather ashamed of my stupidity, and dripping wet as I was, ran all the way to Shields.'

It was a sea whose purity was untouched by pollution except

at the ports, and even there chiefly by animal waste which the natural forces of decay soon destroyed. No detergent residues fostered eutrophication, no oil slicks choked wild life and fouled the beaches, and if strains of *E.coli* capable of transmitting antibiotic resistance existed,[5] the problem they posed belonged to a future undreamt of.

William Thompson was working round the Irish shores at the same time as Arthur was busy, and in the *Catalogue of Irish Zoophytes* which Miss Hunter illustrated, Arthur mentions that Mr R. Ball and Miss Ball of Dublin 'had procured many rare species of zoophytes at Youghal, county of Cork.' He and they were lone reapers in an immense harvest field. How rich that harvest was the following extract from his paper on *Phosphorescence in Zoophytes* discloses:

'Once each week I received from the master of a trawling vessel on the Dublin coast a large hamper of zoophytes in a recent state; in the evening these were taken into a darkened room and the spectators assembled; I then used to gather up with my hands as much of the contents of the hamper as I could manage, and tossing it about in all directions, thousands of little stars shone out from the obscurity, exhibiting a spectacle the beauty of which to be appreciated must be seen, and one which it has been the lot of but few persons as yet to have looked upon.'

Pressed down and running over must the harvest have been to provide popular entertainment every week. Could a hamper load of zoophytes be so readily obtained today? Within a few years, following the immense success of Philip Gosse's popular books on the sea-shore,[6] hordes of amateur naturalists descended on the British coasts and plundered their littoral life almost to extinction.

Zoophytes must be magnified to study their structure, and Arthur's papers are illustrated 'by numerous drawings from the microscope, for which I was indebted to the painstaking pencil of Miss Hunter, a sister of Mrs Alder.'

This is his first mention of the instrument that was to earn him lasting fame. 'As a practical microscopist it is doubtful whether Dr Hassall has ever been surpassed.'[7] Up till that time the microscope had been 'an instrument understood and handled by few, and by such was regarded with much the same feelings as an enthusiastic musician regards his Cremona violin. Now, however, great improvements had been effected in its mechanical construction; and not only had the instrument gained greatly in efficiency and simplicity, but it could be produced at a price so much reduced as to render it possible for any one to purchase one.'[8] How did Arthur obtain one, beg, borrow or steal one? Later, referring to the investigations on which his *History of British Freshwater Algae* was based, he tells us that 'the instrument with which I first worked was a primitive, not perfectly achromatic compound microscope, very trying to the sight.' Was this the same instrument he had used with such formidable results in Ireland? If so, poor Miss Hunter is to be pitied, squinting down the eyepiece as Arthur directed though perhaps she used a Camera Lucida. Arthur did right to acknowledge the perseverance which resulted in the beautiful drawings that illustrated his paper. A quotation from John Hunter, the great eighteenth-century surgeon-biologist, prefaces Arthur's autobiography, but the name is not so uncommon as to suggest she was any relation. More to the point, was she the lady 'distinguished not only for an ardent love of the works of Nature, but as a zealous collector in various branches of natural history on these shores, whose Christian name I have assigned to this new and interesting species—*Sertularia Margarete*.'* If so, it was a timely appreciation by Arthur of her trials with 'a primitive instrument.'

He is vague as to when exactly these researches were carried out, but writes:

'Placed as I was under such favourable circumstances, close to the sea, with its mixed rocky and sandy shore, my old love of nature and natural objects returned with increased force. I soon began to pay almost daily visits to different parts of the neighbouring coast, chiefly between Monkstown and Bray Head' suggesting that they began fairly soon after his arrival in Ireland.

He could certainly have found time for them. All his various activities, walking the hospital wards, winning the Botany prize, and so forth that give the impression of crowded and

---

* Her Christian name was Amelia, her second Christian name may have been Margaret.

strenuous days when compressed into a few paragraphs, in
reality were spread over the five winters and springs, with an
occasional summer, of his apprenticeship during the years
1834–39.[10] In those five half-years, the Candidates' Entry Qualification books of the Society of Apothecaries state that he spent
six months at Jervis Street Hospital and a further six months at
the Mercers Hospital.[11] If six months are added for his midwifery course, and another six months, or a little longer
perhaps, for studying anatomy, his timetable is barely filled up,
not forgetting of course the prime object of his going to Dublin
in the first place, practical instruction in the art and mystery of
the apothecary, learning how to roll pills and make emulsions
that stayed emulsified. It may be noted here that while he was
certainly apprenticed to Sir James 'who had a fashionable
practice in Merrion Square,' the same authority, the Candidates' Entry Qualification Books, state that he was apprenticed
to 'Thomas Murray (either a mistake, or his uncle had two
Christian names) of Lower Merrion Street, Dublin,
apothecary.'[11] At this address there would be a pharmacy
where Arthur filled prescriptions and sold cough lozenges,
embrocation and certainly Murray's Magnesia across the
counter. Possibly he lodged there after his convalescence,
popular opinion would frown on a return to Digges Street. It
cannot be said that Arthur was overworked, a modern medical
student might consider his life a leisurely one, unharassed by
the cytology, embryology, histology, haematology and bacteriology with which the microscope has loaded the present medical syllabus, and he would not have found it difficult to pay
'almost daily visits to different parts of the coast.' Joshua Alder,
his possible mentor, was a specialist in Mollusca and Arthur
may first have gathered shells from the Clontarf sands and
elsewhere. The zoophyte studies, however, it appears must be
attributed to the closing years of his apprenticeship, during the
winter of 1838 and the spring of 1839. He was well-grounded in
the Linnean system of classification which was the foundation
of the Botany courses.[9] No recent text was to hand until the
appearance of Johnston's *History of British Zoophytes* in 1837; and
Arthur mentions that at the time he corresponded with him,
Johnston was engaged in the preparation of a second edition of
his work (published in 1847) in which he makes frequent

reference to Arthur's work. Another pointer in the question of dating is his friendship with James George Allman.

'Amongst the students with whom I was brought into contact,' he writes, 'was Mr George Allman, who like myself had a strong fondness for natural history generally. He also used to collect marine objects and study them afterwards in the evenings at his own lodgings. These evenings we sometimes spent together; we compared notes and described what each had found. The evenings thus spent were very pleasant to me and I have cherished a lively recollection of them through these long years. Allman afterwards became a distinguished naturalist, he published some masterly memoirs on Freshwater Zoophytes and held for a time the Chair of Botany in the University of Edinburgh.'

Allman was far better educated professionally than was Arthur at that time. He was studying to be a physician, and he took his M.D., Dublin in 1840. According to the calendar of the time, in order to take an M.D. a student had to be an M.B. (Bachelor of Medicine) of three years' standing, provided that he already had an Arts degree; no further examination was requisite.[11] Assuming Allman possessed an Arts degree, he must have taken his M.B. about 1837. Students who read for the M.B. degree of Trinity College had to attend clinical lectures at Sir Patrick Duns' Hospital, and it is probable that Allman was far more familiar than Arthur with the instruction of Graves and Stokes and the other great figures of the Dublin school. He succeeded William Allman in the Chair of Botany at Trinity College on 26 March 1844; they were apparently not related, certainly not father and son. George was born in Cork, the son of James C. Allman, and William in Waterford. Subsequently he was appointed Professor of Natural History (not Botany) in Edinburgh University in 1856 as successor to Edward Forbes. He was the author of numerous treatises and papers, is frequently referred to in Johnston's *Zoophytes* while the work he wrote on *British Freshwater Polyzoa* to which Arthur refers was published by the Ray Society.

In 1839 Arthur's indentures expired and he obtained his M.R.C.S., following it up with the Apothecary's Diploma two years later in 1841.

He rings down the curtain on his student days thus: 'My last medical session having come to an end, I had once more to think with the greatest regret of quitting Ireland and of return-ing to England, my permanent home. I was ever most kindly treated in Ireland; I was under great obligations to my uncle and his family and I had to part with many kind friends, especially Mr and Mrs Alder. My pleasant natural history pursuits in Ireland being brought to an end, I paid a last, if not a final farewell to the beautiful Bay of Dublin and its pictur-esque coast scenery, the Hill of Howth, Killiney Bay, Bray Head, Wicklow, with its sugar loaf mountains, the Dargle, the Devil's Dyke, the Meeting of the Waters, the Vale of Avoca and other lovely spots and places within easy reach of Dublin. I may mention here, that I did once return to Ireland for a few days shortly after the Dublin Exhibition, but though the place was the same, the people with whom I was formerly associated were gone, for the most part; some to their last resting place, while others were scattered in different directions. The scenery of course was as beautiful as ever and there were surprising evidences of advancement and prosperity; houses and villas had multiplied everywhere, but especially about Killiney Bay with its charming marine parade.'

Despite the impression this extract gives that he did not return for a great many years, in actual fact he was back again in 1840 after taking his M.R.C.S. in 1839, in order to read the *Catalogue of Irish Zoophytes* that Miss Hunter illustrated to the Dublin Natural History Society on 6 November.

In the quotation from the *Catalogue* that opened this present chapter, he remarks 'I *lately* had the opportunity . . . when on board a Devonshire trawling boat . . . etc.', and he tells us in his autobiography that the trip took place in November. He only ventured once, so it would seem that he went almost straight from the boat to the lecture room. When he first got ashore 'the road seemed to be thrown into undulations and to heave up and down like the sea,' and one trusts that no unsteadiness in his gait aroused unworthy suspicions in the 'Chairman and Gentlemen' to whom he addressed himself.

He closed his address with these words:

'With this paper terminate, I regret to say, my labours in this interesting, and as yet not fully explored, field of natural history. In a few days I shall be called upon to quit the beautiful ocean—beautiful in its strength, its purity, its freshness, its majesty and its infinity; beautiful in calm and storm; and its still more beautiful and ever-varying productions in the study and contemplation of which I so much delight.'

However, eleven years later, on 16 April 1851, he read a joint paper with his cousin John Coppin to the Microscopical Society entitled '*Descriptions of Three Species of Marine Zoophytes,*' so despite his peroration at Dublin he had clearly not lost touch with the subject. He had been elected a Fellow of the Linnean Society by 1851, and he chose to put F.L.S. after his name on the title page, but no professional qualifications. When he read the Dublin paper, he was M.R.C.S. but appears as author simply as Arthur Hill Hassall. In subsequent communications, for example on decay of fruits by fungi, the letters M.R.C.S. do stand after his name.

It is probable that personal business, formalities arising over the expiration of his indentures for example, took him back to Ireland. It was a long and expensive journey to undertake simply for the pleasure of addressing 'Mr Chairman and Gentlemen.' The letters R.C.S.I. appear after his name in the only surviving record of his registration at London University, and presumably stand for Registered at the College of Surgeons of Ireland. I have not been able to find out whether he took any formal examinations, or simply registered with the College, as M.R.C.S. London, but it suggests another reason for his return.

Had he continued to throw as much energy into the study of zoology as he devoted to achieving success in his profession, finding time nonetheless to write his *History of British Freshwater Algae,* he and not J. G. A. Allman might have succeeded Edward Forbes as Professor of Natural History at Edinburgh.

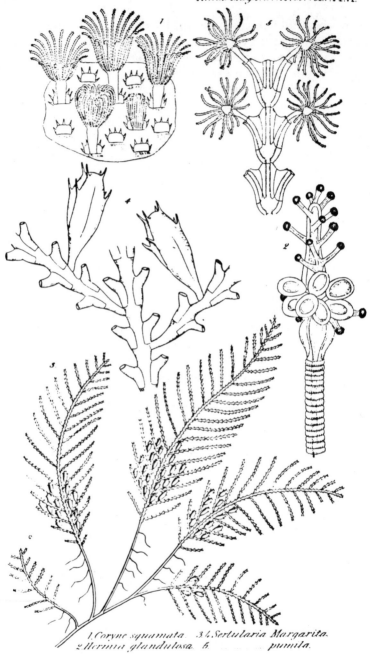

1. *Coryne squamata.* 3.4. *Sertularia Margarita.*
2. *Hermia glandulosa.* 5. *pumila.*

Five illustrations to Hassall's *Catalogue of Irish Zoophytes* 1840–41

'Beautiful drawings by a lady whose name I would willingly mention were I authorised to do so.'' Hassall's zoophyte papers are illustrated by numerous

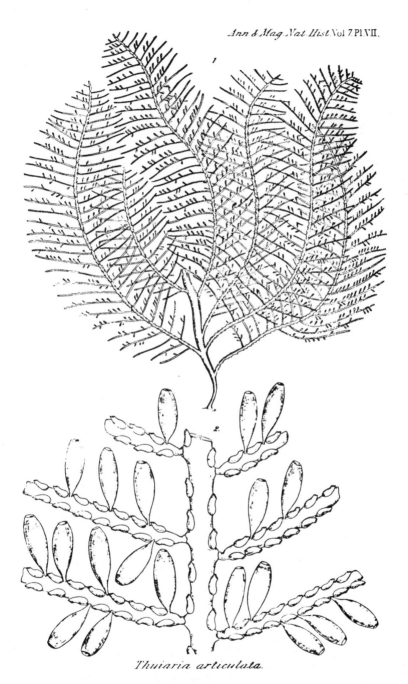

Thuiaria articulata.

drawings from the microscope for which, he later discloses, 'he was indebted to the painstaking pencil of Miss Hunter, a sister of Mrs Alder'.

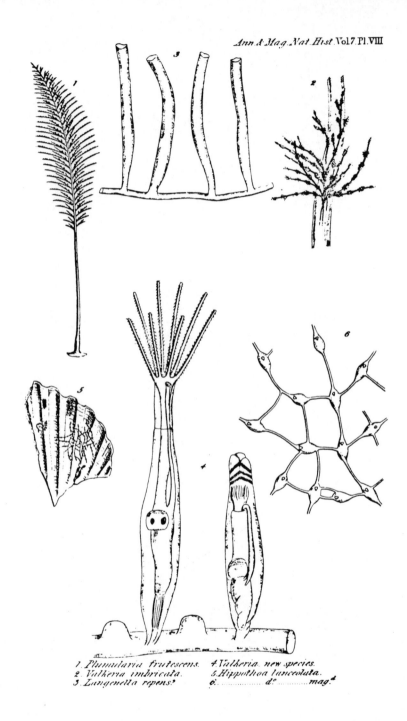

1. Plumularia frutescens.   4. Valkeria new species.
2. Valkeria imbricata.   5. Hippothoa lanceolata.
3. Lagenella repens?   6. .... d°. .... mag.ᵈ

1 Cellepora bimucronata.
2 Lepralia ciliata.
3 .... appensa.
4 .... pedilostoma.
5 .... insignis.
6 .... cylindrica.
7 .... punctata.
8 .... lineoris.

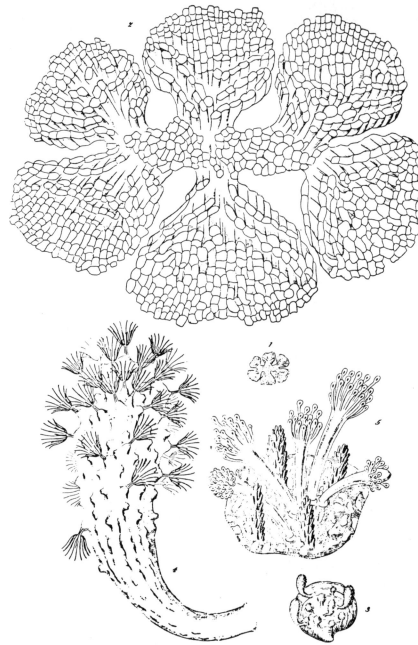

1 2. *Tubulipora lobatula*
3.4 *Alcyonidium hirsutum*
5 *Echinochorium clavigerum*

part rounded ; aperture contracted, circular, with a minute spout-like elongation below; teeth either three or four, surrounding the upper half of the aperture : on either side of the small spout-like elongation referred to, a short blunt process is visible. See Plate IX. fig. 8.—A. H. H.

On stones east of Kingstown harbour, and at the Giant's Causeway : not common.

Membranipora stellata, Thompson. A species has been described by Mr. Thompson in the 'Annals of Natural History' for April 1840, p. 101, under the name of *Flustra* or *Membranipora stellata.* This supposed species I have ascertained to be merely *Membranipora pilosa,* with the bristle abortive, on an expanded surface. I wrote to Mr. Thompson upon the subject, at the same time forwarding specimens for examination, and that gentleman's reply was confirmatory of my opinion. Mr. Thompson was, I believe, the first who described *M. pilosa* to assume the *stellate* form, and to have the cells disposed in the manner indicated in the description of *M. stellata.*

Flustra truncata.—Giant's Causeway, abundant; but not found upon the coast of Dublin.

F. avicularis. This species in a recent state is of a reddish colour, but becomes of a grayish black in drying; this change of colour in drying is, I believe, peculiar to this species, and the cause of it I am not acquainted with. I have sometimes observed the bird's-head appendages (whose motions are so very peculiar and unaccountable) described as belonging to *C. avicularia,* on this species.

I now find that this species is very abundant in Dublin Bay.

F. lineata. Not uncommon on *Patella cærulea* : Bray.

F. tuberculata. Not common : Merrion, Dublin Bay.

F. distans. Polypidom encrusting, grayish, calcareous, reticulated ; cells oval ; margin broad, having its inner edge slightly crenulated ; two short processes are visible at each upper angle of the cells.

I am informed by Dr. Johnston that this species was discovered some years ago by Mr. Bean, but that the habitat of his specimen was unknown. It is on this account, I imagine, that no description of it has as yet been given in Dr. Johnston's 'British Zoophytes.' Dr. Johnston, in a recent letter to me, remarks, "yours is the only native specimen I have seen." From a comparison of specimens of this with *Flustra tuberculata,* I cannot help suspecting that they are in fact one and the same species. When at Belfast a short time since, I saw several fine specimens of this species in Mr. Thompson's cabinet, obtained some time since upon the coasts of Down and Antrim.

On stones east of Kingstown harbour : not common.

F. carnosa. This species, which is undoubtedly no *Flustra,* ought to be raised to a generic rank and placed in the family *Alcyonidulæ.* Pallas asserts (I quote from memory) that the tentacula vary from 18 to 30 : this assertion I am not able to verify, having constantly

References for Chapter Three

1 Arthur Hill Hassall, *Supplement to Catalogue of Irish Zoophytes, with Description of New Species*. Read before the Natural History Society of Dublin, 6 November 1840. Published, with five plates, in *The Annals and Magazine of Natural History*, VII, 1841, 276, 363.
2 Ibid.
3 R. M. Gard, County Archivist, County of Northumberland.
4 Joan Jennings, Royal Irish Academy, Dublin, who also consulted the Natural History Section of the National Museum, the Zoology Department of Trinity College, Dublin, and the Royal Dublin Society.
5 H. W. Smith, *Incidence of E.coli in coastal bathing waters of Britain*, *Nature* (1971) 234.155.
6 Philip Gosse, *The Ocean*, London 1851; *A naturalist's rambles on the Devonshire coast*, London 1853; etc.
7 E. G. Clayton, *A memoir of the late Dr. A. H. Hassall*, Baillière Tindall & Cox 1908.
8 Alleyn Nicholson, *Lives and Labours of Leading Naturalists*, W. R. Chambers, Edinburgh, N.B.
9 W. B. Turrill, *Joseph Dalton Hooker*, Nelson 1963.
10 Elizabeth Gleeson, Trinity College Library, Dublin.
11 C. R. H. Cooper, Keeper of Manuscripts, Guildhall Library.

FOUR
'If Health and Time Permit'

Arthur had very good cause to be grateful to his uncle Sir James, not least for the gift of his indentures. For they served a double purpose. They made it possible for him to train as an apothecary and also to qualify as a surgeon. To quote the Librarian, R.C.S. England, 'As far as Arthur Hill Hassall's apprenticeship is concerned I think that the College would have been perfectly satisfied with his articles; I cannot think that the examiners would have demanded a separate apprenticeship.'[1] Although he had originally trained as an apothecary, yet he took the surgeon's examination first, and obtained the Membership of the College on 24th May 1839.[1]

He tells us that 'before presenting oneself for examination for any of the diplomas it is usual, to ensure fuller preparation and to lessen the risk of rejection, to have recourse for a few months to a special teacher, vulgarly known as a "grinder"; nearly all candidates avail themselves of the services of these gentlemen and it is very necessary that they do so, no matter how diligent they may have been or how well they have prepared themselves. In my day it was well known that several of the examiners of the Royal College of Surgeons held on certain subjects special and sometimes peculiar and crotchety views, with which the examiner was fully conversant.

'If the candidate were unaware of these, his chances of rejection were increased; again, the teacher would test thoroughly his pupil's knowledge, especially with a view to ascertain whether he was prepared in all subjects, or whether there was any one in which he was more or less deficient. The two chief teachers in London at the time to which I refer were Mr and Dr Power, both clever men, admirably fitted for their duties; the work of teaching several hours daily was very exhausting and only strong men could for long periods endure the fatigue and strain. In the classes of these two gentlemen I met with several students who afterwards became famous in the profession of medicine.

'It was as far back as the year 1839,' he writes, 'that I presented myself for examination at the College of Surgeons of England.* I remember very well most of the incidents of the day. It was late in the afternoon that the candidates were ushered into a by no means imposing waiting room, which was vulgarly, but very appropriately, named the "funking room" and the anxiety of the hour or so passed there before being called before the examiners was trying indeed.

'It was curious to note the different ways in which the anxiety manifested itself; some were depressed and silent, their faces bearing evidence of their mental condition; others were unduly excited, but none were at their ease and on all the strain and suspense were manifest.

'One man was very talkative and promised if he passed, he would treat us all to the theatre and afterwards to a supper to celebrate the event.

'At length we were marshalled into the examining room. In this were four small tables, well separated from each other, and at each were two examiners, the candidate passing from one table to the other in succession after being questioned at each for about twenty minutes. The examination was conducted principally by one of the two gentlemen who also took notes of the replies; these were passed on afterwards to the examiners at the next table. In these notes usually some opinion was expressed as to the manner in which the questions, which were wholly *viva-voce*, had been answered, a proceeding which could not fail to exert a considerable influence on the final result, good or bad as the case might be.

'At the first table Mr Anthony White was the chief examiner; he was a friend of my father and I was myself well acquainted with him; this served to put me more at my ease and all went well, but at the next table I was not so fortunate and a difficulty arose as to some point in anatomy, a speciality of the examiner; at the third table nothing very particular occurred. At the fourth table Sir Astley Cooper and Mr Samuel Cooper pre-

* Of London then.

sided. I had always entertained a feeling of admiration and almost of veneration for Sir Astley and I was somewhat taken aback when I found his manner discouraging and calculated to upset the equanimity of a nervous man.

'I remember one of the questions he asked me was: "What in a case of amputation of the foreleg would determine you as to the place where you would make your first incision?" I replied, "The position in life of the patient." "What! Sir!" he exclaimed in angry tones, "do you mean to tell me you would operate differently in the case of a poor and a rich man?" I said, "Yes," not immediately following this up with any explanation, as I was somewhat disquieted.

'Mr Samuel Cooper then most kindly came to the rescue. "You mean to imply perhaps that you would have regard to the man's means of getting his livelihood afterwards?" "Yes," I said, "that is exactly what I did mean. In the case of a rich man I should have more regard to his appearance and needs and should so operate as to allow of his wearing an artificial limb whereas in the case of the poor man I should think more of giving him a good stump to which a wooden leg might be attached, so that he would be able to trudge about and earn a livelihood."'

'"Ah!" Sir Astley then said, "That answer will be accepted!"'

'I had left the table vexed and disappointed, for I had always heard that this great surgeon was remarkable for his urbanity. The answer really required had reference to whether the patient's leg was thin and wasted or stout and muscular; if the former the incision would have to be somewhat higher up than in the latter case, so as to allow of a sufficient covering for the bones. The net result of the examination was that at two of the tables I had acquitted myself well and at the other two less successfully.

'At the end of the examination we were once more ushered into the "funking room", some of us relieved in a measure only of our anxiety. While thus waiting, the examiners were conferring together and deciding upon our fate.

'The first called out, and this was thought to be rather a bad omen, and conducted back to the examining room, was our generous fellow student who had promised us tickets for the theatre and a supper afterwards, in case he passed. In a few minutes he rushed back to us exclaiming, "I am plucked!" He seized his hat, rapidly disappeared and that was the last we ever saw of him.

'In due course we were called collectively before the President of the College, Sir Astley Cooper, and the other examiners and members of the board. Sir Astley, whose grand presence and dignified bearing were so conspicuous, then addressed a few suitable remarks to us; we subscribed our names to the usual conditions of fealty etc. and left the College as fully qualified members; once more free and for a time relieved of such a load of care and anxiety as those can realize who have undergone a similar ordeal.'

Rather unexpectedly, he now plunged into botanical researches at Kew.

'Returning to England for a permanency,' we are told, 'and being once more in Richmond . . . I now directed my attention to the study of structural and physiological botany. In the study of the minute structure of the vegetable tissues I found that the microscope rendered the greatest possible service, indeed it was indispensable,' and there follows the passage on the value of the microscope quoted as the foreword.

'Being at Richmond and in the neighbourhood of the Royal Botanic Gardens at Kew,' Arthur relates, 'I had now the most favourable opportunities of acquiring a further knowledge of botany. Sir William Hooker, the then Director of the Gardens, and Mr Smith were both most kind to me and granted every needful facility; to the latter I had constantly to apply for information, which from his great knowledge and experience he was always able to furnish and although some of my questions were doubtless very elementary he was ever ready to impart the needed help.'

Sir William would raise no objection to his working there, for he had come to Kew from Glasgow where he had held the University Chair of Botany.[2] He would be aware that the regulations for medical students ensured that Arthur had been well grounded in the subject and the Linnæan classification, and that he had received almost verbatim the same instruction from Professor Allman that he had given to his own students, and so far profited thereby that he had won the botany prize. There are letters from Hassall among Sir William's correspondence preserved at Kew, but since Sir William did not take up his post until May 1841 on the resignation of W. T. Aiton, Arthur may have worked under them both, Aiton first and Sir William later.

The numerous papers he subsequently wrote (see list of publications), the greater number on Freshwater Algae but others on such topics as the function of the hairs on the stigma in Campanulaceae, Compositae and other plants (*Ann. Nat. Hist.* VIII 1842.84) or on a peculiar form of spiral vessel found in the Vegetable Marrow, read before the Microscopical Society on 16 November 1842, must be drawn largely from work carried out at Kew during the year 1840–1; although during the latter year he was preparing for his apothecary's examination, which he passed successfully on 21 October 1841.[3] The most striking of his observations, in view of the importance of pollen dating in prehistoric research,[4] are those upon the taxonomic value of pollen grains, published as two exhaustive papers the second of which is profusely illustrated. (*Ann. Nat. Hist.* VIII 1842.92; ibid. IX 1842.544).

Professor Sir Harry Godwin, F.R.S., as doyen of pollen analysis in England, was interested and amused to hear of these early studies by Hassall, of which he was previously unaware. He has remarked that they are not alluded to in Wodehouse's book[5] which deals very fully with the development of pollen-grain morphology as a taxonomic tool. Hassall, he considered, must have been aware of an early comprehensive work by von Mohl (1834) which really laid the foundation for this subject.

And Arthur indeed opens his first paper with the following words:

'On the Continent entire works have been published upon the pollen, accompanied by numerous figures; I allude particularly to Purkinje's work *De Cellulis Antherarum fibrosis* etc.; to that by Fritzsche; and to a memoir by Mohl in the *Annales des Sciences Naturelles*, all of which have appeared within, I believe, the last ten years.'

Furthermore, he published *A Critical Examination of Mohl's views upon the histology of the pollen grain* (*Ann. Nat. Hist.* IX 1842.93) which he concludes by referring to his opinions regarding the pollen grain 'as an assistant in classification.'

About that time there was a sudden burst of interest in pollen

morphology[5] attributable to the improvement in the micro-
scope associated with the names of Jackson Lister, father of
Joseph Lister the surgeon, in England, Chevalier in Paris and
Amici in Italy.[6] 'Soon there arose in every country microscope
makers who produced gradually perfected instruments at a
reasonable price.'[7] Such a one was Andrew Pritchard of 263,
Strand, London, whose photograph may be seen at the Science
Museum, South Kensington.

At the close of his second pollen paper, Arthur acknowledges
his indebtedness to Mr Smith of the Botanic Gardens 'for the
privilege so readily granted of obtaining flowers for the purposes of my enquiry,' and he also remarks, 'my best thanks are
due to Dr Lindley'; he appears later in regard to fungal disease
of fruits and vegetables.

'For the numerous and beautiful drawings which accompany
this communication, all of which have been carefully executed
from rough sketches of my own, made of the object while under
the microscope, I am indebted to the friendship of two ladies,
Miss (Amelia)* Hunter and Miss (Utinia)* Nolcken, who are
ever ready to lend their time and their talents to works of
usefulness; and that not a little of either is requisite in undertak-
ing the drawing of so many illustrations, will be readily
allowed. About two-thirds of them were done by the latter lady
and the remainder by the former.'

So the lady artist who drew zoophytes for him appears once
more. Was she paying a visit to England? Or had she left
Ireland for good? Whatever the reason, it was fortunate she was
at hand to assist Miss Nolcken, for recourse to the microscope
would be necessary to make the pictures accurate.

Hassall may have escorted Miss Hunter back to Dublin
when he returned to read the paper she had illustrated to the
Dublin Natural History Society on 6 November 1840. Or if his
pollen studies were made during the next year 1841 she possibly
travelled back with him from Dublin to Richmond, as guest of
the Hassall family.

Presumably Hassall was still in Ireland on 11 December
1840 when Francis Bauer, botanical painter to George III and
for fifty years resident draughtsman at Kew, died aged 82.

---

* Their Christian names appear on the plates but not in the text.

Arthur would have known him well, the more that Bauer had made numerous pencil sketches illustrating the pollen grains of more than 175 species of plants in 120 genera and 57 families, now bound in a single volume at the British Museum of Natural History. Wodehouse observes that Bauer had an understanding of pollen morphology far in advance of his time.[5]

Arthur must have examined and admired those sketches; though not a professional botanist his own grasp of pollen morphology was advanced for his time. The range of his botanical studies, carried out within a relatively short time, is impressive. They are far from superficial and his contemporaries recognised their quality by electing him a Fellow of the Linnæan Society in 1840.[8] Robert Brown, the famous botanist who had discovered the cell nucleus[6] by use of the microscope, was Secretary of the Society. A medical man who set out in life as did Arthur's father as a regimental surgeon, Arthur must have often seen him at Kew, since Bauer had illustrated much of Brown's work.

On the face of it, all this botanical research appears to make nonsense of Hassall's plaint of restricted means. Had money really been tight, he would have had to get a job the moment he could write M.R.C.S. after his name. (Once Bob Sawyer, the raffish young medico of *Pickwick Papers*, 'passed', friends fixed him up in a practice right away—Sawyer, late Nockemorf.) Yet in Hassall's autobiography we learn of only one serious attempt to find work, in a passage suggesting he had no choice without money but the common lot of becoming an assistant.

'Of course during the time I was engaged on the natural history enquiries and publications above referred to, the question was raised and considered as to my start in life and how I was to turn my professional qualifications to the purpose of achieving an independence. There was no money forthcoming to buy a practice, and to become assistant to another medical man was distasteful to me; hitherto I had pursued much my own way. I was free and my own master and I was disinclined to subject myself to the authority of another. At length Dr Burnes, brother of Sir Alexander Burnes of Indian reputation, became interested in me and gave me an introduction to Sir William Burnett, the then Medical Director of the Navy and the inventor of Burnett's Disinfecting Fluid. Sir William re-

ceived me most kindly, directing me to send in my diplomas
and certificates and said that I should be appointed naturalist
to the *Samarang*, under the command of Sir Edward Belcher, a
great martinet, and which vessel was about to start on a
scientific expedition.'

In Volume IX of the *Annals and Magazine of Natural History*
1842, Arthur's communication, '*A list of Invertebrata found in
Dublin Bay and its vicinity*,' is followed by a description by G. R.
Waterhouse of Carabideous Insects collected by Charles Darwin Esq. during the voyage of H.M.S. *Beagle*.[9] Had Arthur
succeeded in gaining the proffered appointment, a Journal of
the voyage of H.M.S. *Samarang* might stand now beside that of
the *Beagle*, or that of H.M.S. *Rattlesnake* by its former naval
surgeon Thomas Henry Huxley. However, this was not to be. 'I
was rejoiced at the prospect,' he writes, 'as this appointment
seemed the very thing for me. I was a good sailor' (undaunted
by the fate of his brother at sea?) 'and had some knowledge of
marine productions, which for me possessed great charm. I was
kept in suspense a few days only, when a letter arrived request-
ing me to send in another certificate for six months hospital
attendance, as one of those already forwarded could not be
received, that of the Netterville Hospital and Dispensary, an
institution of which Sir James Murray, my uncle was the
founder, owing to its not having the requisite number of beds.'
(The College of Surgeons had raised no objection.)

'This second certificate I was unable to supply and thus the
matter fell through, to my great disappointment. This incident
shows upon what comparative trifles a man's whole career may
depend.' (It was only by a trifle that Darwin sailed on the
Beagle.) 'On my informing my kind friend Dr Burnes of what
had occurred, he wrote congratulating me on what he termed
"my lucky escape." He said the ships commanded by Sir
Edward Belcher were nicknamed "hells afloat" and that in all
probability I should not have been on blue water an hour before
my eyes and limbs would have been—shall I say, not blessed?
The information lessened my regret, as under such provoca-
tion, I might have got into trouble.'

There is another ominous possibility as to why Arthur was
such a slow starter in the professional stakes. He may have been
ill.

By 1839, or certainly by 1840, he should have recovered completely from his Digges Street bout of typhoid. The last sentence in his second pollen-grain classification paper however reads as follows:

'I have now brought to a termination but one of a series of papers which it is my intention, if health and time permit, to publish on the subject of the pollen granule.' *If health permits* – Dr J. N. Blau, speaking of Hassall's middle years, has observed, 'Overwork activated a tuberculous chest lesion, quiescent since Hassall's medical-school days.'[10]

Tuberculosis was so common in those days, affecting one person in seven, that it would not be surprising if Arthur had contracted it. It does provide a satisfactory answer to M.R.C.S. 1839, general practice 1842, three years after he qualified. If health and time permit is a grim conjunction when written by one of his profession.

References for Chapter Four

1 E. H. Cornelius, Librarian, Royal College of Surgeons of England.
2 W. B. Turrill, *Joseph Dalton Hooker*, Nelson 1963.
3 C. R. H. Cooper, Keeper of Manuscripts, Guildhall Library, London.
4 R. G. West, *Studying the past by pollen analysis*, Oxford University Press 1971.
5 R. P. Wodehouse, *Pollen Grains*, Haffner, 3rd printing, 1965.
6 A. Hughes, *A History of Cytology*, Abelard-Schumann 1959.
7 Erik Nordenskiöld, *A History of Biology*, Tudor Publishing Co. New York 1928.
8 T. O'Grady, Executive Secretary, The Linnean Society of London.
9 G. R. Waterhouse, *Carabideous Insects collected by Charles Darwin Esq. during the voyage of H.M.S.* Beagle, Ann. Nat. Hist. IX, 1842. 134.
10 J. N. Blau, *Hassall—Physician and Microscopist*, British Medical Journal 8 June 1968, 2, 617–619.

FIVE

A History of British Freshwater Algae

'During the time of preparation for the two examinations,' e.g.
those of Surgeon and Apothecary, 'my father was residing at
Upper Bedford Place, Kensington. Shortly afterwards we all
removed to Cheshunt in Hertfordshire to be with and help my
brother Richard in establishing himself there; in this, he was, as
already explained, very successful.'

Mr Jack Edwards, Borough Librarian at Cheshunt, has
greatly assisted me with the information that Richard Hassall
had a chemist's business in Turners Hill from 1840–43, his
name appearing on the Jury Lists for those years only. Mr
Edwards adds, 'I have no way of tracing the actual house,
which could have been one of several in Turners Hill at that
time and of which a few have survived. He must have been a
tenant as his name does not appear in the Manorial Court
Rolls, which deal with owners.'

Richard, then, had saved enough out of his school lecture fees
to rent if not purchase a shop and he may have bought the
goodwill of a business. Arthur tells us that 'Attached to our
house at Cheshunt was a large garden, with many fruit trees
and a long high brick wall covered with peach, nectarine,
apricot and other trained fruit trees; such a garden as is still
sometimes found in connection with the older country houses.'

In this connection Mr Edwards looked up some late eighteenth-century maps of Turners Hill and found one or two
houses with large gardens that conform to Hassall's description, although none have survived on their former scale. A quite
possible one is shown in a photograph taken in 1927 showing
the large garden lying behind the chemist's shop and Post
Office, at that time owned by a Mr Gaze. Richard's shop was
certainly close to the cross-roads where a road forks off to the
west from the main road to Waltham Cross as it continues on
down Turners Hill. A little stream runs away eastwards close to

the cross-roads, providing Arthur with a source of material for his studies almost at his back door.

He had hurried to Kew on getting back to Richmond from Ireland, and on arrival at Cheshunt he 'plunged', on his own admission, into studies of freshwater algae which led to the publication in 1845 of a *History of British Freshwater Algae*, a book which has ensured he will be remembered by botanists as long as his own profession will remember that he founded Ventnor Hospital or medical students learn of the 'Hassall corpuscles' in the thymus. It is good therefore to know just where he was living when he embarked on the studies that led to the book's appearance and where his home was while he garnered material now preserved at the British Museum (Natural History) after surviving the vicissitudes of one hundred and thirty years.

The chronology of events however requires some thought. Richard was residing at Cheshunt in 1840 while Arthur was busy at Kew, and during the following year 1841 when Arthur took his apothecary's examination. Next year, in 1842, Arthur put up his plate in Addison Road and started practice on his own. Richard took his External Licentiateship of the College of Physicians of London in 1844, and his M.R.C.S. the same year, after eighteen months' attendance at Charing Cross Hospital. Assuming that his surgeon's examination was early in 1844, (Arthur had been examined on 24 May 1839), then he must have been riding up to the hospital from Cheshunt just as Arthur describes: 'he used to start on horseback at 5 o'clock in the morning, returning in the evening in the same way' during the whole of the year 1843 and for six months in 1842. The examination for his Extra-licentiateship was academic compared to any Arthur had so far taken, and his self-education for his school lectures must have proved indispensable.

'He was admitted an Extra-Licentiate of the College on 28 June 1844. By this time there was a written examination for the licence of the College, which comprised three parts, papers in therapeutics, physiology (including anatomy) and pathology, together with translations from Greek and Latin. The statutes appear to make no distinction between the Licentiates who could practise throughout England, including London, and the Extra-Licentiates who could practise elsewhere in England but not in London or within a radius of seven miles. After the passing of the Medical Act, 1858, the College made bye-laws which gave Licentiates and Extra-Licentiates who had taken their diploma before 1858, the opportunity to be registered as Members of the College. This Arthur Hassall did in 1875 but Richard did not avail himself of this opportunity.'[1]

When he left Cheshunt, Richard went back to Richmond, and married a Mrs Gibbons. After her death he married Miss Alicia Goddard, daughter of Archdeacon Goddard, 'by whom he left four children.' The obituary in the *British Medical Journal*[2] which supplies this information further observes 'he was an excellent practitioner, cautious without timidity, a warm-hearted friend, and a kind, good, faithful and earnest man in all things.'

His entry to the earliest (printed) *Medical Directory* of 1847 is as follows:[3]

'Hassall, Richard, Richmond Green, Surrey. External L.R.C.P. 1844, M.R.C.S. Eng. 1844 and L.S.A. Medical Officer, Richmond Dispensary.'

(L.S.A., Licence Society of Apothecaries, is confusing since he was not examined and approved by the Society until 29 December 1849. Note M.R.C.S. England; the Royal College of Surgeons of London to which Arthur was admitted in 1839 became R.C.S. England by charter in 1843.)

By 1859 Richard's entry includes the further information:

'M.D. St Andrews 1842; late Surgeon, 1st Royal Surrey Militia; Fellow Medical Society of London. Author *Cholera its nature and treatment, Poisoning by Chloride of Zinc.*'

He had succeeded his father as surgeon to the Surrey Militia and still later, as we learn from Boase's *Biography*,[4] he became Examining Physician to the Ventnor Hospital, so the brothers were associated professionally in the years that lay ahead of them at Cheshunt.

In order that his sisters might keep house for him, the Hassall family perhaps moved to Cheshunt in 1840, leaving Arthur to pursue his studies at Kew.

When he went to Addison Road in 1842 he writes that 'my father and my sister Eliza accompanied me.' There is no mention of Ann, who possibly remained at Cheshunt until Richard wound up his business there in 1843. Where was Richard then between 1843 and 1844, when he took his ex-

Arthur Hill Hassall aged about 45; mezzotint by S. Marks, after a photograph by Mayall. Behind him is the silver statuette awarded him for his services to public health; by his left hand the Ross microscope with which, in his own words, 'many vastly important facts were to be brought to light', and the books it enabled him to write, *British Freshwater Algae* and *Human Microscopic Anatomy*.

The chemist's shop on
the right, in the village
of Cheshunt, Herts, is
possibly the site where
Richard Hassall had his
apothecary's establish-
ment, and could there-
fore be the original
house with the large
garden behind where
Arthur Hassall carried
out his experiments on
fungal decay of fruits

The unknown subject of
this charming picture
wears Regency dress —
the big sleeves went out
of fashion in 1836, two
years after Hassall sailed
to Ireland to begin his
medical studies. It could
be a portrait of one of
the young ladies who
illustrated his papers on
natural history

Norland Villa, Addison Road North (originally no.32, now no.37),
London. Here Hassall brought his first wife Fanny Augusta du
Corron, and here he wrote his *History of British Freshwater Algae*, the
Microscopic Anatomy of the Human Body, and his first pamphlet on public
health, *Observations on the Sanitary Condition of the Norland District, etc*. In
one of the bedrooms he bled himself by candlelight to obtain relief
from pleurisy

Two separate herbarium sheets from Hassall's collection of British freshwater algae at the British Museum photographed side by side (actual size), *Mougeotia notabilis* on the right and *Draparnaldia plumosa* on the left. The label for *M.notabilis* appears to describe both specimens, an unfortunate juxtaposition ex Herb. A. H. Hassall

[A. H. Hassall MS.]

Myriactula botatilis

Watson Hill

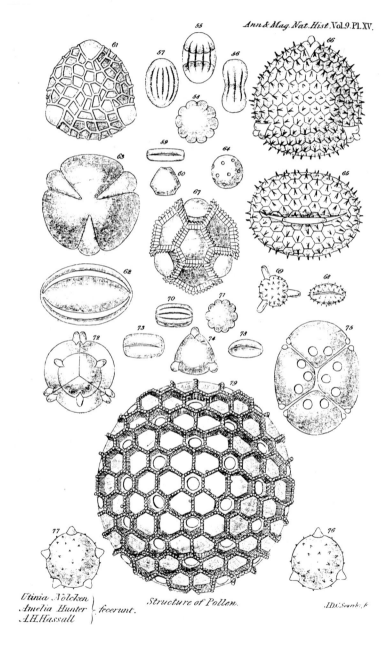

Utinia Nölcken
Amelia Hunter } *fecerunt.*
A.H. Hassall

Structure of Pollen.

J.D.C. Sowerby, fe

Taxonomic tools: one of Hassall's plates of pollen grains drawn from his own sketches by Amelia Hunter and Utinia Nolcken

The Ventnor Hospital
shortly before it was
pulled down

Hassall aged 62 (from a
photograph), after he
had left England for the
Italian Riviera and writ-
ten a guide to San Remo

The portrait by Lance Calkin that was formerly in the dining-room of the Ventnor Hospital and now hangs at the entrance to the Hassall Ward of the Newport Hospital, I.O.W.

aminations after riding up every day for eighteen months to Charing Cross Hospital? And who looked after the shop while he was away all day at the hospital? Hassall Senior? Ann and Eliza could not be trusted to distinguish between calomel and corrosive sublimate. When the family went to Addison Road, an assistant must have been engaged. Arthur was roaming the countryside in search of his confections.

'Not having at the time any clear views as to the future, I had now a period of comparative rest and leisure which however did not last very long. Hertfordshire, as is well known, is on the whole a damp county, abounding in little streams, dykes, ditches and ponds, some perennial.'

This on the debit side, perhaps, but it is also the county of Charles Lamb and of Samuel Lucas the artist of Hitchin, the little market town where young Joseph Lister went to school about the time Arthur was settling down to his medical studies in Dublin. (His great surgical contemporary was exactly ten years his junior.)

'In my walks about in search of . . . interesting organisms,' writes Hassall, 'it occurred to me that (these) growths, green, olive-coloured or yellow, often seen floating on the surface of ponds, or diffused through the water beneath the surface, would be very interesting, instructive objects for the micro- scope . . . They are of a vegetable nature, the freshwater types of the seaweeds or Algae. At this time comparatively little was known of the Freshwater Algae; there was no separate work treating of the subject; so here was a field for investigation which promised a rich harvest to the diligent seeker.'

He had first examined them at Kew, and he explains: 'The Freshwater Algae are divisible into three distinct groups: the *Diatomaceae*, characterised by siliceous shells . . . and the *Desmi- diaeceae*, green, soft, non-siliceous . . . had been studied at an earlier period than the filamentous *Confervae* to which my attention was more particularly directed.'

Thus preoccupied, he can seldom have been seen in the shop, except on those occasions when he found the counter an admirable work bench in intervals between handing over sticks of liquorice or pennyworths of Glauber salts, or delving into the special jar where the leeches lived. Doubtless his sisters would have been happier had he kept out of the way altogether, for

muddy footprints improved neither shop floor nor stair carpets.
'My search for freshwater algae led me to all sorts of low-lying,
damp, marshy, and wet places; to ditches, dykes, ponds, pools,
lakes, reservoirs, rivers and cascades; indeed wherever water or
even humidity was to be found, as damp walls and buildings,
within a radius of several miles around Cheshunt. On many of
these occasions I got very wet; indeed I seldom returned home
without wet feet, as at times it was necessary to go into the
water.' We learn that getting wet on algal forays brought on
most painful neuralgia, which got worse after the local doctor
treated it with calomel. 'The treatment was changed, tonics
and plenty of nourishment being substituted; under this regimen, as was to be expected, I soon recovered.'

His first communication on algae (*Ann. Nat. Hist.* IX
1842.431) took him back once more to Dublin, to read *A Sketch
of the Freshwater Confervae* before the Dublin Natural History
Society on 1 November 1842. Six more communications followed in the Annals between 1842–3, while on 6 December and
20 December 1842, and 7 February 1843, he read before the
Linnæan Society an Essay on the *Distribution, Vitality, Structure,
Modes of Growth and Reproduction and Uses of the Freshwater Confervae.*

He broke off his investigations to take his Apothecaries'
examination, where botany proved an unexpected ally, on 21
October 1841.[3] 'For the purpose of this examination,' he
writes, 'recourse was again had to the very useful but somewhat
abused "grinder". After due preparation I found myself before
the examiners of the Company. Of one incident of this ordeal I
have a clear recollection. I was asked to give an illustration of
the rapidity and force of the growth of vegetable cells and
tissues. I cited the case of fungi, some species of which, I said,
had been known in the course of a single night to raise up and
disarrange even heavy flag stones. "Ah indeed!" exclaimed the
examiner; he beckoned to two or three of the other gentlemen
present and related to them what I had stated; they all seemed
incredulous and I was getting uneasy, as it seemed to me that
the gathering round of several examiners portended no good.

'At length he said "You have told us a pretty tale, pray Sir,
where did you get it from?" I replied "You will find it related in
Gilbert Burnett's *Outlines of Botany*", a voluminous and noted

work not often in the hands of a medical student. The manner of the examiners changed, and in the end I came off with flying colours and was complimented.'

Once this hurdle was over, the algal studies were apparently resumed with all their former zest. As he himself observes, 'I was now a fully fledged medical man and duly qualified to hold most public medical appointments.' He had explained earlier in respect of the dual system of training that 'in order legally to hold certain appointments in the Army and Navy, in the Poor Law Service and in many other public offices, it is necessary to hold the double qualification.' Why, then, had another year to pass before he turned his professional qualifications to proper use and began to practise? What was he living on meanwhile, and who paid for the trip to Dublin? Whatever the explanation, he was able to round off his studies, and subsequently 'the whole of the articles and the results of further researches were collected and incorporated in two volumes, one of text and one of plates, in a work entitled *A History of the British Freshwater Algae*. This was published by Longmans in 1845; it was dedicated to James Scott Bowerbank, F.R.S., a great and deserving authority in those days on microscopical subjects whose weekly gatherings at that time I frequently attended. Fifty years have elapsed since the investigations were made on which this work was based. I refer to this remote date because looking back now by the light of the present day, no one can be more conscious than myself of the many defects of these volumes, both of the text and the illustration. The instrument with which I first worked was a primitive, not perfectly achromatic compound microscope, very trying to the sight. The one hundred and three plates were all executed by myself, both the drawings and the engravings. If I could have had the opportunity of investigating the subject again and bringing out a new book, what a very different affair I should be able to make of it with modern instruments and other advantages now attainable!'

The Preface informs us that this crude instrument had happily been replaced by a Ross microscope, and it is of great interest to be told also 'that he was deeply obliged to a lady for the devotion of much time to the shading of many of the plates.' Scrutiny of the particular plates reveals that her name was Fanny du Corron, whom he married. 'I must not forget,' he writes, 'to acknowledge the literary assistance I have derived from Mr Coppin, of Trinity College, Cambridge.' (Years later another Trinity graduate, Franklin Lushington, was to prove a staunch friend of his widow.) Arthur and his cousin perhaps strolled round Great Court, discussing style and grammar; a jaunt to Cambridge would have been a pleasant excursion from London, and possibly Fanny accompanied him. Among those to whom he expresses thanks are Sir William Hooker, the Reverend M. J. Berkeley and Dr G. J. Allman, 'my highly valued friend, and talented Professor of Botany in the University of Dublin,' so the friendship begun in student days had not lapsed; Allman had held the Chair of Botany for just a year when Arthur wrote. The Reverend M. J. Berkeley, whose name appears again in the list of subscribers (he put his name down for three copies), figures prominently in some further Cheshunt researches described in the next chapter. Other subscribers 'whose generous patronage has relieved my mind of considerable anxiety' are Professor Balfour, Professor Allman, and Dr George Johnston, his zoophyte mentor. Richard's name also appears, although he might have merited a presentation copy for finding house-room for the author while he pursued his investigations.

The text is lucidly written, and has the nostalgic charm of Victorian works on natural history penned for more leisurely days, while certain plates have the added attraction that they are signed by his future wife.

Clayton, writing in 1908, mentions that the book was reprinted more than once during Hassall's lifetime; later editions appeared dated 1852 and 1857, and the generic name Hassallia proposed by Berkeley in 1845 has been applied successively to various algae by observers belonging to three different nationalities; by Berkeley in 1845, by Count Vittore B. A. Trevisan (1848) and by Bornet and Flauhaut (1886–8).

What do professionals say of this work today, a hundred and thirty years after it was published?

In 1927 the late Professor Fritsch, a noted authority, remarked:

'One of the earliest attempts to bring together all that was then known concerning British algae was Dillwyn's *British Confervae* which appeared in 1809; hardly any further advance was made in this country until the publication in 1845 of Hassall's *History of British Freshwater Algae*.[5]

Dillwyn appears as one of the subscribers to Hassall's book.

Recently, Mr E. A. George, M.A., former Director of the Culture Centre of Algae and Protozoa, has found time to give me a specialist opinion:

'It is difficult for one who started his study of the algae almost exactly a century after the publication of Hassall's *History of the British Freshwater Algae* to give a valid assessment of this work. Hassall's was the first comprehensive British Algal Flora which enabled the reader to identify algae as far as was possible at that time. It was essentially a work of compilation rather than of original research, though it is obvious that Hassall had more than a casual knowledge of his subject, because many of his records are the first for Britain.

'There can be no doubt that Hassall did much to help and encourage the amateur microscopists who were so characteristic of the mid- and late-Victorian era. Professional algologists were few and far between in those days but there is little evidence that Hassall played any great part in shaping the course of algology other than perhaps providing a pattern for Cooke when he wrote his *British Freshwater Algae* forty years later.

'Hassall's contemporaries, Ralfs, Kützing, Naegali and Rabenhorst, all of whom published their major contributions just after Hassall's book appeared, are now generally regarded as being among the founders of modern scientific algology.

The first comprehensive Flora of British Freshwater Algae therefore as Mr George and Professor Fritsch agree, was published by Hassall. The priority important in scientific history must go, not to a professional botanist, but to a young doctor whose health appears to have been dubious, and who was twenty-eight years old when the book was first published. Had Hassall been a professional botanist and concentrated on the algae, it may safely be assumed that his text would now be numbered with those founders of algology mentioned above. His book was the first in England in its field, Cheshunt the scene of his labours, and it is frequently mentioned in his papers on the subject, more so perhaps than other localities. *Zygnema* were very common in the district, perhaps more abundant than other species; and near Cheshunt, 'in a pond whose waters are perennial,' he met with several fine species of *Plumatella repens*, that would catch his eye as freshwater representatives of the marine zoophytes he had studied in Ireland.

The considerable and representative collection of freshwater algae Hassall made was offered to the British Museum (Natural History) six months after he died on 9 April 1894, by Edwy Clayton, the executor of his will. Writing on behalf of Mrs Hassall the second (Hassall married twice), then resident at San Remo, to W. Carruthers, F.R.S., Keeper of Botany at the Museum, from the Chemical Laboratory, 43 & 44 Holborn Viaduct, on 21 November 1894, he explained that the collection had been in his keeping for some time past. 'It is not bulky, there are some 150 specimens mounted on large sheets of paper and labelled with names and localities as a rule; and there are also perhaps 100 more specimens in little paper packets and on pieces of glass.'

The Museum accepted the collection, which totalled 883 specimens representing confervoid algae and herbarium specimens of diatoms. Today, a hundred and thirty years after it was made, it comprises about 150 microscope slides and a number of the original herbarium specimens. A great many of the slides were made in the 1890s, presumably from Hassall's original tube material of which none appears to have survived. Most genera of confervoid algae are represented from a wide variety of sources, including Ireland. Some are Hassall originals, while others are from Mr Jenner of Tunbridge Wells to Hassall or to Jenner from Hassall ex Cheshunt and Notting Hill.

I was privileged to be shown the confervoid algae collection by Mrs Jenny Moore of the Museum's Department of Botany. I am most grateful to her for the photograph taken of two of the herbarium specimens and to Mr Ross, Keeper of Botany, for permission to reproduce it; chosen for their associations are *Batrachospermum plumosum* from Cheshunt and *Mougeotia notabilis* from Notting Hill.

It is not at all surprising that when the collection finally arrived at the Museum some specimens were dirty and others lacked collection details. The marvel is that so much had survived intact during Hassall's frequent changes of residence in the fifty years that elapsed between its formation and

Clayton's letter to the Museum. It is not unique, of course, Mr Ross points out. The Museum has some other algal collections, for example Kützing's collection of diatoms made between the late 1820s and the 1850s, and the herbaria of about 6000 specimens made by Hassall's contemporary Edward Jenner (died 1872), although Hassall's might claim special notice since it was made by the author of the first comprehensive work on British Freshwater Algae. When so much else relating to him has been lost, where is his Ross microscope now? Most of all, where is the silver statuette publicly presented to him on 4 May 1856 (see Chapter Eight)? Hassall's collection grows more precious with the passing years and posterity owes a great debt to Edwy Clayton for his faithful stewardship.

References for Chapter Five

1 L. M. Payne, Librarian, Royal College of Physicians, London.
2 *British Medical Journal*, 1 January 1876.
3 C. R. H. Cooper, Keeper of Manuscripts, Guildhall Library, London.
4 Frederick Boase, *Modern English Biography*, 1851–1900, Vol. 1A–H, Frank Carr 1915.
5 Fritsch and West, *A Treatise on the British Freshwater Algae* by the late G. S. West, New and Revised Edition by F. E. Fritsch, Cambridge 1927.

SIX

Fungi Rotted the Potatoes

The Hassalls' large garden at Cheshunt with its high brick wall and fruit trees, was the theatre of some further remarkable studies that have been undeservedly neglected.

'While I was engaged on the Algae,' Arthur records, 'my attention was directed to the subject of decay of fruits and some kinds of vegetables . . . The garden had many sorts of fruit trees . . . I thus had abundant material for my observations.'

He reported his findings in a series of six papers. One was read to the Linnæan Society on 20 December 1842; four to the London Microscopical Society, the first on 19 October 1842; and the last on 19 April 1843; while the sixth was published in the *Annals and Magazine of Natural History* (XII. 1843.86). To these may be added a letter on the Irish Potato Murrain to the *Bristol Mercury*, Saturday 4 October 1845, reproduced at the end of the chapter. He carefully distinguishes between the ordinary kind of decay or destruction 'occurring in over-ripe fruits which had so far passed their maturity that they could scarcely be said to be living, but were to be regarded rather as dead matter and therefore subject to ordinary decay and decomposition'; and the other kind of decay, of a totally different character, 'observed to attack fruits in different stages of growth and of diverse structure and consistency, which it was observed began as a spot only.' According to the consistency of the fruit the spot increased in size somewhat rapidly; it was usually of a brown colour, and between the affected and unaffected part of the fruit there is always a well-marked boundary line. Recourse to the microscope revealed that 'in the unsound portions of the fruit the component cells were separated and disclosed by the penetration of the branched thallus of a species of fungus.'

He went on to inoculate sound, recently gathered fruits with the fungal thallus, and also 'apples, pears, peaches and several other kinds of fruits while still growing on the tree.' Lettuces and the potato received similar attention. 'As far back as 1841 I published in newspapers and elsewhere the fact that the potato disease was occasioned by the growth in the tuber of a fungus, *Peronospora infestans*.'

Fruits were also infected by the inoculation of spores.

'Living fruits may be inoculated by other means than the introduction beneath the skin and epidermis . . . many fungi produce an aerial fructification and produce a multitude of spores so small and light that a puff of wind scatters them and they are so minute that they readily enter the fruit through any broken surface . . . Nor do I discard the notion of the entrance of sporula by the stomata or spongioles . . .'

Hassall answered the criticism that the fungi might be the result and not the cause of the decay by pointing out that the particular decay only followed introduction of decayed matter containing fungal thalli, or of fungal spores.

Ehrenberg had infected sound fruits from decayed ones at the turn of the century, and Hassall had clarified the position. It might be claimed that he had satisfied Koch's postulate that the organism must be found in all cases of the disease.

He could not satisfy the further postulate that the organism must be responsible for the disease after it had been maintained in pure culture for several generations. This was a refinement beyond the technique of Hassall's day. Spallanzani at the close of the eighteenth century and Dujardin during the first decades of the nineteenth had been defeated by the inherent difficulties, which were highlighted very dramatically by a recent TV series *Microbes and Men*. A French team studying cholera in Alexandria in 1883 tried in vain to isolate the responsible vibrio in liquids in flasks, while success was achieved by a rival German team led by Robert Ludwig Koch using the solid media he had devised. Had Hassall turned his original and versatile mind to the problem, he might have solved it in time for his own cholera researches during the epidemic of 1853 and anticipated Koch's triumph by thirty years.

The Rev. M. J. Berkeley was the British authority on fungi at the time Hassall carried out his studies of fungal disease. He had completed the whole of the Fungus volume of J. E. Smith's *English Flora* in October 1835 and from 1836–43 issued his

British Fungi. Between 1834–49 he contributed descriptions of
36 Algae to the Supplement to *English Botany* vol. II–IV, after
he published in 1833 a monograph *Gleanings of British Algae.*
Hassall corresponded with him; there are letters of his among
the Berkeley correspondence at the British Museum (Natural
History). Hassall of course thanks him in the preface to his own
book on Algae, to which Berkeley subscribed.

Three years after Hassall published his results, in 1845, the
Potato Murrain broke out in Ireland. The Great Famine
followed as the potato crop failed from fungal disease, and
nearly brought down the Government. ('Rotten potatoes have
put Peel in a great fright,' growled the Duke of Wellington.) Drs
Lindley, Kane and Playfair were appointed by the Government
to enquire into the cause and 'they were only too glad to avail
themselves of Mr Berkeley's invaluable assistance.' Thus ori-
ginated Berkeley's first contribution to plant pathology which
conclusively controverted the prevailing view which Lindley
voiced: 'I am perfectly satisfied that fungi do not *cause* it; though
God knows they follow it fast enough.'[1]

Berkeley only reluctantly came down on the side of the
angels:

'After an attentive consideration of the progress of the disease
and of almost everything of value that has been written on the
subject, and after duly weighing the peculiar difficulties with
which it is attended, I must candidly confess that with a
becoming share of philosophic doubt where such authorities
are ranged upon the opposite side, I do believe the fungal
theory to be the true one.'[1]

Even so, he still hedged. 'The reports are so contradictory
regarding the subject of contagion, that it is impossible to build
anything upon them. I have seen no evidence of contagion in
the experiments I have myself instituted.'[1]

Nonetheless, E. C. Large[2] is of the opinion that in advancing
the hypothesis that a living parasitic organism on the potato
foliage was the cause and not the consequence of the Potato
Disease, the Reverend Berkeley was anticipating the Germ
Theory of Pasteur by nearly a quarter of a century 'The issue,'
says Large, 'was the establishment or rejection of a new
conception of disease, not only in plants but ultimately in all
living things.'

But Hassall had anticipated Berkeley. Writing in retirement years later, he pointed out:

'The foregoing inoculation experiments were made as long ago as 1841–42 and taken in conjunction with some further observations of mine to be detailed later (i.e. upon cholera). They are of special significance in relation to the more recent and precise investigations and discoveries which have thrown such a flood of light on the diseases of both the vegetable and animal world.' His reports dealt with disease from an aspect that was novel for his day, in a wider context than he met on his professional rounds, and they suggest he had in mind a new concept of the vexed problem of contagion. 'They are alike,' he suggests modestly, 'of practical importance and scientific interest.'

He had provided hints of how the Potato Murrain might have been checked when he exhibited to the Microscopical Society on 16 November 1842 an apple inoculated with fungus where decay had been remarkably slowed down by coating the apple with sealing wax varnish. He also suggested that apples and pears might be preserved by packing them in boxes filled with lime.

The late Professor F. T. Brooks, F.R.S., Professor of Botany at Cambridge, first learned of these studies of Hassall's from the present writer. As a mycologist, who had re-edited the 10th edition of D. H. Scott's *Flowerless Plants*,[3] he considered Hassall's work to be of the greatest importance, and that it merited far wider recognition than it has hitherto received; Hassall must take priority over Berkeley in the field of phytopathology, if not in that of mycology.

Supplement to the *Bristol Mercury*,
Saturday 4 October 1845

Correspondence

To the Editor of the Bristol Mercury

Sir – I have read with regret various notices which have appeared in the papers of late announcing the failure, in certain districts both in this country and on the continent, of the potato crop. Numerous inquiries have been instituted with a view to ascertain the causes of the decay which affects both the stems and the tubers, and many explanations have been offered to account for it, but none that I am acquainted with give the true exposition of the phenomenon.

In several papers published in the *Transactions of the Microscopical Society of London*, some two or three years ago, I showed that the decay to which fruit and vegetables, especially the softer kinds, are so subject is, in nine cases out of ten, not a natural process, the result of the chemical action of the elements of dead organic matter on each other, but is the consequence of the growth throughout the cellular tissue of the thallus, or root-like portions, of several minute species of fungi, the presence of which may be easily detected by the aid of an ordinary microscope.

The *modus operandi* of the fungus is as follows: The exceedingly minute sporules (which are analagous to the seeds of plants of higher organisation) transported by the air, alight on the surfaces of the fruit or vegetable about to become affected, and finding entrance by some small abrasion or aperture, speedily throw out their thousand rootlets; these penetrating in all directions between the cells effect their separation; the cells thus isolated become the subject of chemical action, and rapid decomposition is the result.

In the paper referred to, I showed also, that the disease might be communicated to sound and healthy fruit and vegetables by inoculation, and to these also while still attached to the tree or growing in the ground. The inoculation may consist of the introduction into the fruit or vegetable, the subject of the experiment, of either a portion of decayed vegetable matter containing the thallus, or roots, of the fungus, or simply of the sporules or seeds themselves.

The operations of the fungus are at first confined to the interior of the fruit etc. affected; and the fungus is itself, of course, at that time invisible to the eye; its presence, however, is known by the remarkable softening and discolouration which attends its growth; at first seen as a small spot, the extension of which can be detected hour by hour, until at last the entire fabric of the fruit is involved in destruction. Ere long, however, the cuticle or skin of the fruit decomposes, so as to allow of the external development of the fungus, which is then manifest in the form of mouldiness on the surface, and which consists almost entirely of the sporules, which are so exceedingly small and light that the slightest breath of air can waft them far and near, again to be deposited on some devoted crop, whose destruction (small agents as they are) they are capable of effecting.

Now, the fungus or fungi (for many species are capable of producing the same result) which I have described as occasioning the decay – in nine cases out of ten – of fruit and vegetables, is also the cause of the destruction of the potato, a fact to which allusion was made by me, some three years ago, in the paper cited above, which it seems to me is not generally known, and which is moreover capable, to a certain extent, of practical application.

The great predisposing cause to the development of the fungus, the source of all the mischief, is the long duration of rain and damp; our efforts, therefore, should be directed first to the endeavour to counteract, as far as possible, a wet state of the soil; and this may be done by strewing the earth with lime, by exposing the tubers to the free action of air, and by the removal of redundant arm or stalk; and second, to the adoption of every means whereby the sporules or seeds of the fungus may be destroyed. Thus all affected potatoes should at once be burned, and on no account should tubers procured from any district in which the disease has manifested itself be used as seed.

Sound potatoes it is probable might effectually be preserved in lime.

The diseased tubers, although rendered useless for human food, may be given in any quantity to cattle, without producing any pernicious result; at least, such is the experience of several persons who have made the trial. I do not consider that there is the slightest foundation for the report that the potato tuber is worn out, and I therefore treat as chimerical the notion that this all-important vegetable will, in the course of a few years, become extinct.

The importance of the subject will, I hope, be considered as a sufficient apology for the length of this letter.

Yours etc.

Arthur Hill Hassall, F.L.S.

Norland-villa, Addison Road North,
Notting-Hill, Sept. 29th, 1845.

References for Chapter Six

1 M. J. Berkeley, *Observations, Botanical and Physiological, on the Potato Murrain*, J. Hortic. Soc., London, Vol. 1, pp. 9–34, 4 plates, 1 text figure, 1846.
Together with selections from Berkeley's *Vegetable Pathology* made by the Plant Pathology Committee of the British Mycological Society, Phytopathological Classics No. 8, published by the American Phytopathological Society, 1948, East Lansing, Michigan.
2 E. C. Large, *The Advance of the Fungi*, Dover Publications Inc., New York 1962.
3 D. H. Scott, *Flowerless Plants*, Tenth Edition re-edited by F. T. Brooks, A. & C. Black 1932.

SEVEN

The Thymic Corpuscles of Hassall

Hassall records finding the alga *Mougeotia* in pools among brickfields at Notting Hill (*Ann. Nat. Hist.* Vol. X 1843.34). The district therefore was not unknown to him when he decided, or it was resolved at a family council, to start practice on the Norland Estate. Hassall henceforth; Arthur had attained man's estate.

It was not a salubrious neighbourhood, since close by were the notorious Potteries, marshy brickfields populated by 'pig-keepers, soap-boilers, gypsies and tramps,' but he would meet with little professional competition on a new estate, and it was conveniently close to Kew and to Richmond, so that the family could keep in touch with Richard after he returned there.

'It was determined,' Hassall relates, 'that my father, my sister Eliza and I should remove to some likely new suburb of London, take a small house there and that I should commence practice. This plan was carried out. A corner house was secured in Addison Road North, on the Norland Estate, Notting Hill. I succeeded in obtaining a fair general practice and on the death of my father aged 73, I removed to a larger villa in the same road.'

Miss Medwyn Barnes of the Kensington and Chelsea Central Library had little difficulty in finding where Hassall put up his plate and a red lamp over the door. 'A red lamp, projecting over the fanlight of the street door, would have sufficiently announced the residence of a medical practitioner.'*

To quote her letter in full:

'It would appear from the ratebooks that Arthur Hill Hassall occupied No. 32 Addison Road North and the adjacent shop. These properties were on the corner of Addison Road North and Queensdale Road. No. 32 is now 37 Addison Avenue.

'Addison Road North was newly built and Hassall appears

---

* *Pickwick Papers*

as the first tenant in the second rate of 1843 and the shop (originally placed in Queensdale Road) appears by 1845. Hassall's occupancy of No. 32 appears to date from this year's second rate and the shop would appear to have been his first dwelling, but I cannot be quite sure of this as so much new building was taking place in the road at this time. However the Post Office London Directory for 1845 lists his address as No. 33 while subsequent years give it as 32, so this would appear to confirm a change of residence.

'Hassall is last listed in the second rate of 1849. No. 37 Addison Avenue is still standing and forms one of a pair of pleasant early Victorian paired two-storey houses. Their design has been attributed to F. W. Steat and they form part of the Norland Conservation Area.'

No. 33 must be 'the small house in a new suburb of London to which my father, my sister Eliza and I moved from Cheshunt' and 32, now 37, the corner house where Hassall moved after his father died. The Post Office Directory furnishes independent confirmation of a change of residence and also that Hassall Senior died in 1844, 'a year or two after I began practice in 1842.'

No. 32, now 37, Addison Avenue, is a pleasant dwelling, in a pleasant locality not far from Holland Park Road and Royal Crescent, quite a substantial semi-detached house with an area basement in front and a small square garden at the back, where a wistaria is now trained against the house wall. Hassall called it Norland Villa, perhaps to please his bride. For on 26 May 1846, he married Fanny Augusta du Corron, spinster, at St Pancras Church, describing himself as 'Surgeon.' Her father is described as 'Gentleman': he was presumably of independent means.

Broad stone steps lead from the street to a front door glass-panelled today but possibly of oak when a brass plate engraved *Arthur Hill Hassall, Surgeon* in flowing script was screwed to it. The customary red lamp hung over the door, or that of the adjoining shop, and at normal times, when not ill with pleurisy, Hassall probably slept in the front bedroom above the hall, where he could throw up the window sash to speak to midnight callers waiting anxiously in the street. The cream-painted hall with an arch would be the same as in his day, and of the two rooms opening off it, one would be a dining room, and the other a combined consulting room and study, a microscope by Ross standing under a bell-jar in the window as its most conspicuous feature. (Hassall used it so constantly he probably possessed one of the special low microscope tables introduced to compensate for the long body of those early instruments.)

It was in this house, while busily engaged in practice and in studying for the London University M.B. he took in 1848, that he wrote *The Microscopic Anatomy of the Human Body* with the original description of the famous thymic corpuscles, and also his first essay in Public Health, *Observations on the Sanitary Condition of the Norland District, Shepherds Bush and Pottery with suggestions for its improvement*. Both were published from Addison Road in 1849.* Not only for these remarkable pioneer studies, the *Microscopic Anatomy* was the first book in English on the subject, but for all Hassall's public services in questions of food adulteration and sanitation (and not forgetting the foundation of the Ventnor Hospital) No. 37 Addison Avenue richly deserves a commemorative plaque upon the wall stating that Arthur Hill Hassall once lived here.

The shop that Miss Barnes mentions that adjoined No. 32 and may have been Hassall's first dwelling is in the tradition of his day. In poorer districts especially a doctor's shop was the rule, and one lingered down into the 1930s in the Hampstead Road, London, a few minutes walk from Warren Street. With the framed diploma hung in the window and the plaster horse displayed among brightly coloured medicines, it was a replica of that over which Mr Rawkins presided, in Albert Smith's story *The Adventures of Mr Ledbury*, published in 1851.

'The medical establishment conducted by Mr Rawkins was situated in one of the streets which would be intersected by a line drawn from the New River Head to Clerkenwell Green . . . essentially a doctor's shop with a red bull's-eye lamp over the door . . . distinguished from a mere chemist's and druggist's by the Apothecary's diploma framed in the window which was set out with a great eye to display with elegant arabesques of teeth

---

* The '*History of British Freshwater Algae*' may also have been published from No. 32.

on black velvet tablets . . . packets of soda powder in blue and white envelopes, brightened by the dusky red of pitch plasters and the doubtful white of the plaster-of-paris horse occupying the centre pane. There were, also, announcements in gold letters upon glass slips, similar to those seen at pastrycooks, except that they notified BLEEDING and PATENT MEDICINES instead of ices and ginger beer . . .'

Hassall tells us that 'my patients were of two classes, well-to-do people, the occupants of good houses and villas, and workmen with their families, living chiefly in the Latymer Road and in the notorious and insanitary Potteries.'

Dickens' addicts will immediately recognise on the one hand the Veneerings and on the other, Mr Toodle the engine driver, who rattled Mr Dombey and the ineffable Major Joe Bagstock down to Leamington Spa.

The Veneerings of course would only take notice of a brass plate on the door, but Mr Toodle and his dependants looked for a doctor's shop. Nothing so fancy perhaps as Mr Rawkins' establishment, but a shop would be expected, and Hassall doubtless advertised BLEEDING in gold letters on a glass slip.

Bleeding, by the lancet or leeches, was in those days the universal panacea. Hassall bled himself when ill with pleurisy at No. 32 'with marked and immediate benefit and relief.' On the subject of bleeding he writes, 'I was in attendance upon an elderly retired physician; it was a very severe case of erysipelas of the head and face; the attack not progressing favourably, he expressed a wish to see an old friend, a distinguished London surgeon. He ordered a copious bleeding from a full stream, and this order was repeated several times, chiefly on the grounds that the blood abstracted after being set aside for some time exhibited the contracted or "cupped" surface and the "buffy" coat of which in those days one heard so much. I had my own scruples as to these repeated bleedings, but being by far the junior I felt constrained to obey orders. Formerly bleeding was in many cases no doubt carried too far, now it is not as frequently resorted to as it should be. The relief afforded in suitable cases is immediate and well-marked, and no equally effective substitute for the practice has yet been devised.'

It is not surprising that Hassall acquired 'a fair practice'. Clayton, who was the Executor of his Will and knew him for many years, informs us that 'he was distinguished by a grave and courteous manner'[1] and he would approach each patient with the same thoughtful interest he employed in identifying different genera of sea anenomes or algae, an interest, not a clinical detachment, which would be warmly appreciated. He would go his rounds on foot, hiring a horse only when necessary from one of the livery stables as common then as garages today. It was tiring physically, but possibly he was spared mental anxiety, since things just could not be hurried. A critical case might resolve itself before he got to the bedside, the sufferer was either dead or had got over the worst by the time a breathless messenger had reached his house and brought him back. Still, the urgency would irritate a nature that approached a problem cautiously, and he did find practice 'harassing. I had much midwifery and a good deal of night work.' (As Bob Sawyer – late Nockemorf – put it to his crony Benjamin Allen in *Pickwick Papers*: 'They knock me up at all hours of the night; they take medicine to an extent which I should have conceived impossible; they put on blisters and leeches with a perseverance worthy of a better cause; they make additions to their families in a manner which is quite awful.')

The microscopy meetings held every week by James Bowerbank no doubt provided a welcome escape, and his thoughts would turn to microscopical human anatomy. By 1840 classes in microscopical anatomy were held in the medical schools at both London and Edinburgh.[2] The subject was not compulsory, and Albert Smith draws the picture general in the great London hospitals in his novel *Christopher Tadpole* (1848) when that Old Hand Mr Barnes warns a New Hand (very raw, fresh up from a country apprenticeship) 'that if he was shown the globules of the blood circulating in the tail of a fish, he'd best look sharp and get a peep before the fish expired on the demonstrator.'

The older men who taught Mr Barnes would have agreed with Dr Kidd, who after examining a delicate morphological preparation under the microscope, 'made answer first, that he did not believe it, and secondly that if it were true, he did not think that God meant us to know it.'[3] It was the attitude of a mind fighting a lost battle when increasing numbers of anatomists were seizing the opportunity afforded by the new microscopes to puzzle out the minute structure of tissues. Continental observers had got off to a flying start, although as Hassall pointed out 'our observers have (not) been idle but the results of (their) labours have not, as yet, however, been embodied in a separate work; some of them have been mixed up with works on descriptive anatomy and physiology.'

In 1846, once the move to 32 Addison Road was safely accomplished, Hassall writes: 'As soon as I was settled in my new home, I determined to apply the microscope to some subject of more professional interest and of wider and more general importance. I therefore commenced the examination of some of the tissues of the human body and being charmed and fascinated by what I saw, resolved to microscopically examine systematically all the fluids, tissues and organs of the body; a task of no common labour, one which would occupy much time, years perhaps, and which had not hitherto been accomplished in its entirety; certainly not in this country.

'To carry out this design effectually, it was necessary that I should make constant visits to the post-mortem room of a Hospital and should engage a competent artist. I was therefore present at a great many autopsies at St George's Hospital and I engaged the services of a Mr Miller, a microscopical draughts-man. He was a most intelligent young man and he rapidly became, aided by his natural ability and constant employment, exceedingly proficient.

'In this way I examined all the structures and organs of the body and I ultimately resolved to bring out a separate work on the subject.

'The results of this application of the microscope culminated in the publication of certain papers in the Lancet in the years 1848–49, the names of which will be found in the List of Publications, and in 1852 in the production of a work, in two volumes, entitled *The Microscopic Anatomy of the Human Body*. One volume consisted of text, the other of plates, mostly coloured by hand, or printed in colour, embracing upwards of four hundred illustrations all drawn by Mr Miller from my preparations; many of these were engraved by him on stone and others by Mr Lens Aldous and Mr S. W. Leonard, both very skilful micro-scopical artists.

'The prime purpose of this work was to give faithful illustrations of the minute structure found in the liquids and solids of the body as revealed by the microscope; it did not pretend to trace the origin and development of the several tissues and structures, but was mainly limited to the one purpose named; even with this limitation, looking back over the pages I am conscious it contains some errors and omissions, but the plates are, as a whole, I believe unrivalled even to this day, though forty years have passed since their publication. My work was the first complete book in the English language devoted to this subject and though so long out of print, so far as I am aware no work of similar extent has yet appeared in this country, but German and American editions of my *Microscopic Anatomy* were afterwards published.'

Looking back over the pages, it is apparent he mistook the date. The title page bears the date 1849, not 1852, and the preface, in which he states the work took 'three years of more or less constant labour' is dated 27 July 1849, at Notting Hill. He must presumably have collected all the data for his *History of British Freshwater Algae* at No. 33 Addison Road (although it bears the address Norland Villa, Addison Road North, Notting Hill), and the move to No. 32 was followed by the publication of *The Microscopic Anatomy*. Hassall dedicated the work to Thomas Wakley, M.P., the formidable iconoclast who had edited the *Lancet* since its first number appeared on 5 October 1823, and very shortly their friendship was to lead to one of the most dynamic associations in the history of medicine, marking a milestone in the story of public health in England.

In the preface, Hassall writes 'to Mr Andrew Ross, as on a former occasion, I have to express my obligations, Mr R. having at all times furnished me with any information I might require, as well as provided me with any necessary apparatus,' the former occasion being in the preface to *A History of British Freshwater Algae*. Andrew Ross, who had worked with Professor Barlow, made lenses to Lister's design, and by the middle of the nineteenth century they had become popular.[4] In conjunction with Wenham he also introduced the binocular microscopes in this country. His microscopes are described in Jabez Hogg's *The Microscope*, 15th edition 1911. One of his earliest microscopes appeared under the name of Andrew Pritchard, who was mentioned in Chapter Four. Pritchard published an English translation of Ehrenberg's *Die Infusionthierchen* in 1841, which was reviewed in the *Ann. Nat. Hist.* Vol. VIII 1841 1 IV Supplement, and became a standard text for more than thirty years until succeeded by Saville Kent's *Manual of the Infusoria*. Hassall must certainly have had a copy of Pritchard's *Infusoria* at his elbow when he later made his water pollution studies, and his first 'primitive, not perfectly achromatic instrument' might have been one of Pritchard's earliest and cheapest models.

To return to his histological studies, Hassall in examining the thymus noted some peculiar particulate bodies. 'Each separate adult thymus is constituted of numerous, probably some hundred, follicles . . . the "milky fluid" contained in the follicles and reservoir is made up, to a great extent, of an immense number of granular nuclei, as well as numerous cells of large size, which do not appear hitherto to have been either described or figured in a satisfactory manner . . . many of these cells contain several granular nuclei, each of which is surrounded by one or more concentric lamellae. . . .'

These cells of large size were named by F. G. J. Henle, C. G. Lehmann and others the concentric corpuscles of Hassall, briefly The Hassallian Corpuscles, familiar to generations of medical students. The copy of Sharpey-Schafer,[5] 1920, which I used as a student, states that 'within the medulla, but never in the cortex, are found peculiar concentrically laminated bodies (concentric corpuscles of Hassal)' – one *l* be it noted.

In 1853 Hassall drew attention to some large compound bodies 'as large as pus corpuscles' which he first encountered in cases of cystitis and 'upon which Lehmann bestowed the name "Hassall's Corpuscles".' Certain vegetable structures were also thus called after his exposures of food adulteration, but I have been unable to trace the reference.

'In the latter half of the nineteenth century,' writes J. N. Blau in the *British Medical Journal*, 8 June 1968, 'the eponymous title of "Hassall's Corpuscles" was also attached to the cellular deposits in the urine of patients with cystitis. Today it is confined to the lamellated bodies unique to the medulla of the thymus. Arthur Hill Hassall is remembered by the unique thymic corpuscles which bear his name.'[6]

The function of the corpuscles for long remained obscure, but

lately they have received much attention, and the same authority asks:

'How would Hassall have reacted to recent knowledge
gained as to the behaviour of his corpuscles? He would surely
have been interested in their waxing and waning in size with the
involution of the thymus, in their active uptake of antigens and
antibody from the circulation, as well as their storage of
gamma-globulin in healthy human beings at all ages and in
patients with myasthenia gravis and rheumatoid arthritis.
However, why these bodies occur only in the thymus remains a
mystery. It has been postulated that they play a part in
long-term immunity, a function which no doubt would have
appealed to Hassall's keen interest in preventive medicine.'[6]

Hassall had taken a first vigorous step along that road of
preventive medicine by publishing in the same year, 1849, the
pamphlet previously mentioned, on the *Sanitary Condition of the
Norland District*. 'The Potteries at that time were very notorious,' he writes, 'and were in close proximity to the best part of
the Norland district; the site had formerly been a brick-field,
the numerous excavations made never having been filled up
and hence there were many collections of foul and stagnant
water. The population was of a very low class and included pig
keepers, soap boilers, gypsies, tramps, beggars, etc.; the place
abounded in piggeries and being without drainage, was in so
insanitary a condition that it was rife with disease and a
constant danger to the neighbourhood. I drew up a full report
on its condition and this contained a curious illustrative map, in
which each of the many stagnant pools and ponds, ditches and
other sources of danger were delineated. This was my first effort
as a Sanitary Reformer; but it was not destined to be my last by
many.'

After firing this warning shot, if a nautical metaphor be
permitted since Hassall was fond of the sea, he fired a ranging
shot, a *Memoir on the Organic Analysis and Microscopical Examination of Water supplied to the inhabitants of London and the Suburban
Districts* in the columns of the *Lancet*.[7] Then to continue the
metaphor, in the same year, 1850, he let fly a full salvo: *A
Microscopical Examination of the Water supplied to the inhabitants of
London and the Suburban Districts*, illustrated by twelve coloured
plates. This is a remarkable study, and Hassall's description of

the Thames makes the flesh creep.

'The organic matter and other impurities of the Thames water exist in more than microscopic quantities.

'Let the observer walk along the banks of the river for a short distance and the following will, in most instances, be the result of his observations:

'In one spot he will notice the carcases of dead animals, rotting, festering, swarming with flies and maggots, and from which a pestilential odour proceeds, contaminating the air around; in another, he will see a variety of refuse borne along by the lazy current of the stream – decaying vegetables, the leaves and stalks of cabbages, grass from a new-mown lawn, excrement; in another, he will remark the commotion of the water, occasioned by the bubbling up of some noxious gas; and still further on, he will perceive some sewer, discharging its corrupt and filthy contents (consisting of the mingled refuse of, perhaps, a whole town or district) into the bed of the river, causing the water round to assume an inky blackness.

'Should the tide happen to be out, the observer should abandon the towing path, take a boat, and row to some of the shallower parts of the stream. If here he plunges his hand into the water, he will bring up a dirty and slimy mass; this, examined microscopically, will be found to consist of *dead* organic matter, together with vast numbers of *living* animal and vegetable productions.

'Entire acres (I might say without exaggeration) of a substance similar to the above may frequently be noticed on the recession of the tide.' This repulsive liquid formed most of the water supply of London.'

Hassall wrote in retirement:

'London and its vicinity were formerly supplied by ten Water Companies; five of these supplied water from the Thames, and the other five from the River Lea, the Ravensbourne, the New River, the Hampstead Ponds, and deep wells in the chalk near Plumstead, respectively.

'The names of the Companies drawing water from the Thames were, The Grand Junction, The West Middlesex, the Chelsea, The Southwark and Vauxhall, and the Lambeth.

'Of the five Companies which took their supplies from the

river Thames the intake of one was at Kew Bridge, one at Hammersmith, two at Battersea and one at Lambeth, that is to say from the most polluted portions of the river ... It was assumed, that the water as delivered to the consumers, had undergone an efficient process of purification, either by *precipitation* in special reservoirs, or by *filtration*, or by both processes combined.

'So imperfectly were the processes of subsidence and filtration carried out, that the water of most of the companies, as delivered for use and consumption, was more or less opalescent and discoloured and when set aside for some hours, a deposit visible to the naked eye and sometimes considerable in amount, consisting of mixed organic and mineral matter, always subsided.'

This pamphlet is remarkable because it reveals Hassall once again as a pioneer, drawing conclusions from his own observations far in advance of his time. To quote a recent authority:

'All categories of living creatures are useful in the study of pollution. For severe organic pollution, ciliates and other microorganisms are useful; for less severe cases or pollution of other types the larger invertebrates and the algae are useful.'[8]

In fact the plates in Hassall's pamphlet illustrate this clearly, although they were drawn a hundred and thirty-two years ago, and demonstrate indisputably, as the text explains, that in waters moderately polluted, collected from Brentford say, or the Hampstead Ponds, Entomostraca and diatoms are conspicuous at the expense of ciliates – 'animal productions'.

The latter however teem in grossly polluted waters to the virtual exclusion of all plants except Blue-Green algae.

'The predominance of vegetation in the water from Brentford,' writes Hassall, 'and of animal life in that procured at Lambeth (a wine bottleful collected two hours after the steam boats had ceased to ply) struck me as so remarkable that I was induced to make a series of observations on the river water, both upwards and downwards, in the course of the river from London. These have brought to light the fact that Thames water, from Brentford in one direction to Woolwich in an opposite, swarms with living productions of the genus *Paramoecium* and of one species of this genus, the *P.chrysalis* of Ehrenberg in particular. These animalcules exist in such vast

numbers, that a wine bottleful of the water obtained in any
condition of the river, at high or low tide, is sure to contain large
numbers of them. They are met with in greatest abundance
close to London and in the neighbourhood of the bridges where
the sewers open.'

He was in fact using *Paramoecium* as what is now called a
Pollution Indicator. He understood clearly why *Paramoecia*
were found in greatest numbers close to the bridges where the
sewers opened; his conclusion that 'they found in pollution
their means of subsistence and growth' marks the first tacit
recognition of the dependence of certain ciliates on a supply of
bacteria rather than green algae as a source of food.[9]

Hassall's observations were largely made on the Thames,
and until recent years they were only paralleled by those of
Lackey in 1938 on ciliates as pollution indicators in the Scioto
River.[9]

Hassall did not fail to point out that the river reaching
London had already received sewage from Oxford, Reading,
and Henley-on-Thames, and suggested that as a source of
water from London, the Thames would be improved by diverting their waste elsewhere. His method was 'to take samples of
the water of the Thames from Kew in one direction to London
Bridge in the other, also from the mains of the different
companies and from the supply pipes and cisterns of various
houses supplied by each of the companies. A certain quantity
was set aside in suitable vessels to allow any solid matters which
they might contain to subside; after some hours these residues
were subjected to a searching microscopical examination.'

Who, may one ask, took the samples? It was a physical
impossibility for Hassall, busily engaged in practice, to collect
them all personally, often from a considerable distance. What
explanation was given to the householders whose cisterns they
wished to plumb, by the Victorian originals of those representatives who call today, armed with an untidy sheaf of papers
clipped to a board? He would naturally prefer, with his scientific bent, to take as many as possible himself, but a wide circle
of friends and acquaintances must also have been recruited,
and his assistant Mr Collins knocked up again to go and collect
some more.

The microscope revealed crude sewage—'threads of cotton

and wool, animal hairs, bile-stained half-digested scraps of meat' – not only in the Thames residues but in those from water delivered by the companies drawing water from the Thames, the Southwark and Vauxhall and the Lambeth Companies being by far the worst offenders.

'I well remember,' writes Hassall, 'one special occasion on which I demonstrated this was after a dinner I gave when residing in Bennet Street, St James's, at which Dr Farr, Dr Dundas Thomson and other well-known sanitary authorities of the day were present.

'Great dissatisfaction was (then) entertained of the existing water supply' and the 'horrible significance of these revelations' caused a public outcry.

'Mr Edwin Chadwick was in 1850 the Chairman of the General Board of Health; he sent for me and wrote down my evidence at some length; especially that relative to the organic impurities and contaminations in the waters supplied by the Metropolitan Companies. The evidence will be found in Appendix iii of the Board of Health. Mr Chadwick was greatly pleased with the results I detailed of the microscopical examination of water and stated that my evidence was just what he had been seeking, as the chemical details relative to the organic matter rendered so little help in determining the question of the purity and wholesomeness of water and the production of disease through the drinking of impure water.

'The Board of Health was at that time greatly occupied with the question of the Metropolitan water supply . . . while condemning the then supplies of the metropolis, the Board recommended a new source, namely the Bagshot Sands . . . it was proposed to place one of the reservoirs on Wimbledon Common, a position sufficiently elevated to allow one half of London being supplied with a high-pressure service.

'Of course this proposal encountered fierce opposition on the part of the Water Companies and hence the Ministry of the day were led to appoint three Commissioners, Professors Graham, Miller and Hoffman to make a separate and independent examination and to report on the subject.'

The following year, 1851, Hassall was chief witness at a Parliamentary Committee of Enquiry into the Metropolitan Water Supply, presided over by Sir James Graham, Bart.[10]

'Before this Committee I was summoned on the part of the Government; I was sitting quietly near Mr Phinn, Q.C. (acting for the Government) when one of the opposing counsel crossed over from his side and addressing Mr Phinn asked him whom he was going to take first. "Are you going to examine that humbug, Dr Hassall?" This of course brought me to my feet and when I told him who I was and requested an explanation, he was not a little taken aback, apologised, begged I would not take his remark seriously and said it was meant as mere banter between counsel, as I was a hostile witness. Mr Phinn essayed to quiet the storm and to throw oil on the troubled waters. I did not receive the explanation very graciously nor did it improve my frame of mind for the subsequent examination. I afterwards learnt that the barrister in question was Mr Macauley.

'After the examination-in-chief was finished, Mr Sergeant Bellasis proceeded to cross-examine me. I will remark at the outset, that his manner and the wording of some of the questions put to me were such as ought not to have been adopted towards a scientific witness, present at the inquiry in the discharge of a public duty, and whose desire was to speak the truth only. It was a manner, which seemed intended to discredit and intimidate. The first question put was "Where do you live?" Luckily my address was a good one or the inference might have been unfavourable. Mr Bellasis was very particular in his enquiries as to the bottles in which the samples were collected; "Were they clean?" "How did I know they were clean?" "Did I wash them myself?" and on my replying that I doubtless did so if necessary, he said, "You are a bottle washer, then!" The idea that all the creatures found in samples of impure water could possibly be derived from the bottles used, whether clean or dirty, was of course in itself absurd. However, Mr Bellasis made the most of his case and exerted himself zealously on behalf of his clients. It was evident, that he had studied my book on the *Microscopical Examination of the Water supplied to the Inhabitants of London* and had noted the passages which seemed best suited to his purpose; he picked out what he deemed its weak points, he put wrong constructions and drew inferences not fairly justified by the text and did his very best to damage my evidence. This however he certainly did not succeed in doing; on the contrary, by his cross-examination and

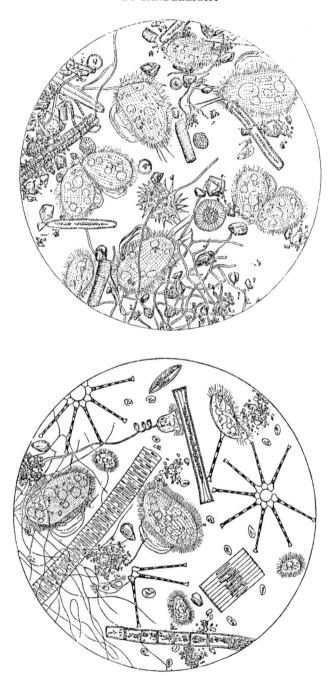

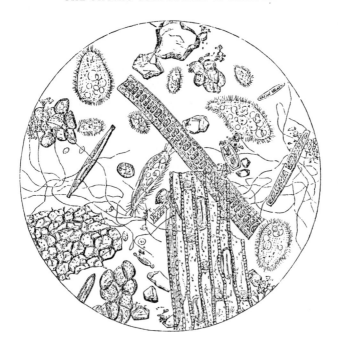

London's Drinking Water in 1851

Three of Hassall's drawings with the Camera Lucida, magnified 220 dia-
meters, showing the ciliate protozoa, notably the *Paramoecium chrysalis* of
Ehrenberg, he adopted as pollution indicators because he believed 'they
found in the pollution means of substance and growth'. *Top left*, in water
supplied by the West Middlesex Company, *bottom left*, in the Thames at
Waterloo Bridge, *above*, in water supplied by the Chelsea Company. 'The
samples of water from which the engravings which illustrate this Report have
been prepared, were obtained either from the Thames itself, or from service
pipes, in February 1851.'

persistence he confirmed and added force to the facts telling against the quality of the water supplied to the inhabitants of London.'

A later report *On the Microscopical Examination of the Metropolitan Water Supply*, addressed to the Right. Hon. William Cowper, M.P., President of the General Board of Health, in 1857, appeared among the Parliamentary papers of that year. (See list of publications.)

In the same year Hassall was also author of a *Report, Microscopical and Chemical, on the Water of the Serpentine*, drawn up at the request of Sir Benjamin Hall, Bart., M.P., presented to the House of Commons and ordered to be printed (1857).

In 1852 an Act was passed requiring the Water Companies taking water from the Thames to collect it in future from above Teddington Lock. They were allowed five years to make the removal.

When cholera broke out again in London in 1853 and reached a peak of mortality in the following year, the Lambeth Company had already moved to Teddington but the Southwark and Vauxhall had not; and the inhabitants of houses supplied by the latter company suffered eight times as much as those supplied by the better water of the Lambeth Company; the number of persons who died in the houses where the impure water was drunk was three and a half times the number who died in the houses where the purer water was supplied.[11].

The *Lancet* observed in 1851 that 'the true interpretation to be placed on the presence of infusoria in water was not well understood until Dr Hassall called particular attention to the condition of animalcular life in Thames water near London . . . This inquiry belongs to the naturalist, the physiologist and the microscopist, and to Dr Hassall is due the honour of having first applied the resources of these, extensively, and in a practical as well as a scientific manner, to an examination of the actual condition of water in general, and particularly the state of that now in use in the Metropolis.'[12]

'In a practical as well as a scientific manner' – that is how he made immense capital of his discovery. Not that his Report on the Serpentine rang down the curtain on his activities in relation to a clean water supply. The list of his publications shows that as the acknowledged authority on the subject he was consulted on many subsequent occasions.

During the cholera epidemic of 1854 a massive Board of Health Report on the *Microscopical Examination of Different Waters*, illustrated by 25 coloured plates, was drawn up and presented to both Houses of Parliament by order of the Queen (1855); and as late as 1878 three Reports with engravings on the Sanitary State of the Thames appeared in the *Lancet*.[13]

A month after Hassall died, his widow Alice Margaret wrote to the Earl of Rosebery, then President of the Ventnor Hospital, that his labours had earned for her husband the title of public benefactor, and she placed first among them 'his researches and investigations which were the means of procuring a new water supply for London.'

References for Chapter Seven
1 E. G. Clayton, *A Memoir of the late Doctor Arthur Hill Hassall*, Ballière Tindall & Cox 1908.
2 Arthur Hughes, *A History of Cytology*, Abelard-Schumann 1959.
3 W. Tuckwell, *Reminiscences of Oxford*, London 1907.
4 F. W. Palmer and A. B. Sahier, *Microscopes to the end of the 19th century*, Science Museum Illustrated Booklet, H.M.S.O. 1971.
5 Edward Sharpey-Schafer, *Essentials of Histology*, Eleventh Edition, Longmans 1920.
6 J. N. Blau, *Hassall – Physician and Microscopist*, British Medical Journal, 8 June 1968, 2 617–619.
7 *Lancet*, 1850, 1.230.
8 H. B. N. Hynes, *The Biology of Polluted Waters*, Liverpool University Press 1960.
9 E. Gray, *The Ecology of the Ciliate Fauna of Hobsons Brook*, a Cambridgeshire Chalk Stream, J.gen.Microbiol. 6 108–122, 1951.
10 Reports of Commissioners 1851 Vol. XV – Minutes of Evidence taken before the Select Committee on the Metropolis Water Bill, p. 227.
11 Priscilla Metcalfe, *Victorian London*, Cassell 1972. See also Jephson, *The Sanitary Evolution of the Metropolis*, 1907.
12 *Lancet*, 1851, 1.188.189.
13 *Ibid.* 1878, 526.562.601.

EIGHT

'Adulteration the Rule, Purity the Exception'

'I continued to practise at Notting Hill,' Hassall remarks, 'till about the end of 1849, when an event occurred which changed the whole of my future life . . . Walking home from one of the London theatres I got wet through, pleurisy followed, my life was in danger . . .'

Few G.P.s would have found the energy to walk into London after the day's grind, and if it suggests Hassall went his rounds on foot and eschewed a carriage, could he not afford a coach home when it started to rain? The pleurisy perhaps was a blessing in disguise and if his life was in danger, the enforced inactivity came none too soon. He had been driving himself remorselessly, physically and mentally. If any home ever deserved the cliché 'a hive of industry', it was 32 Addison Road. Over and above practice 'with much night work' writing the *Microscopic Anatomy* and the *Norland Report* (the former calling for many visits to autopsies at St George's Hospital), any one of them occupations that would have filled up an ordinary man's day, he had been reading for the degree of M.B., Bachelor of Medicine, at London University.

There were two examinations for the M.B., the second two years after the first.[1] 'As I had been in practice for so many years,' Hassall explains, 'I was permitted by the regulations to undergo the successive examinations at much shorter intervals than is permissible in the case of ordinary candidates, the actual examinations being the same in all cases.

He went on to take the M.D. of the University, he says, three months after obtaining the M.B., but this is clearly a mistake.

He was M.B. in 1848 and M.D. in 1851, three years later.[2] This accords with the regulations that stipulated an M.B. of the University had to put in five years in practice unless at the second examination he had been placed in the First Division when 'two years of practice will be dispensed with.'*

We learn that the examinations for the M.B. and M.D. 'were formidable affairs, each occupying many hours for several days . . . the ordeal was much more searching than I had anticipated.'

In the same year 1851 he took further examinations to become a Member of the Royal College of Physicians of London (M.R.C.P.). 'I remember that the examiners were very polite and considerate and that this was the only instance in which I had to undergo any classical examination and this was confined to translating some sentences from the work of a certain Latin author.'

Candidates for the London M.D. be it noted were examined not only in medicine but also in Elements of Intellectual Philosophy, Logic and Moral Philosophy, to add a polish to the final product and ballast to medical theory.

Meanwhile 'the locality (Notting Hill) was bad and did not suit my health, the soil was of clay, I determined to part with my practice and make a fresh start elsewhere.' He sold the practice to Mr William Benjamin Hemming, Surgeon, who continued the practice for some years.

'I removed in 1850 to Park Street, Grosvenor Square.' Surprisingly 'after my life was in danger' into the London smog; into the London of the *Morning Chronicle* survey of Labour and the Poor by that special correspondent Henry Mayhew: 'Have you read the *Morning Chronicle*,' Douglas Jerrold asked Mrs Crowden Clarke in 1850, 'these marvellous revelations of the inferno of misery, of wretchedness, that is smouldering under our feet? We live in a mockery of Christianity that, with the thought of its hypocrisy, makes me sick.'[3] Into a London whose Art was dominated by the Pre-Raphaelite Brotherhood who had attacked the metaphorical fog they considered obscured the Royal Academy; twenty years later Luke Fildes depicted the misery of the poor in his searing *Applicants for Admission to a Casual Ward*, sensation of the Academy of 1874. Into the London, too, of Cholera, festering during 1848 and 1849 in the slums behind the elegant façades of Belgravia, its progress

* Regulations for these degrees from the University Calendar for 1851 are given in the Appendix.

nervously watched by Dr Southwood Smith, Chief Medical Officer of the Board of Health which the cholera had brought into being. In the parishes around the Elephant and Castle in the autumn of 1849 bells tolled continuously while empty coffins were delivered like parcels on the heads of running men who knocked on doors like postmen.[4]

Hassall must surely have read the book published in 1849 *On the Mode of Communication of Cholera*. The author made a suggestion it might be spread by the water supply. He was a Yorkshire farmer's son who had walked up to London and established himself in a practice in Soho. As a young medical student aged eighteen he had fought a serious outbreak of cholera in a mining village single-handed. His name was John Snow.[5]

Mr Hemming cannot have paid a great deal for the practice, since Hassall had not been long enough in Notting Hill to establish a wide connection. And what did Fanny think of the upheaval? Much of what Mr Hemming paid would go on the expenses of moving and setting up a new home, and money must have been tight unless her father helped them out. It was a desperate gamble to put up his plate again right in London where competition would be keen, unless he picked up a death vacancy. Was she still alive? Was there a young family? Hassall is silent, and we can only speculate on ways and means. All we are told is that about that time complaints in the Press about the quality of coffee caught his eye – more than Mayhew's articles it would seem, although of course his experience of the miseries of the poor in Dublin and the Potteries began where Mayhew's left off.

Despite financial problems, despite professional claims on his time and all his water pollution studies described in the last chapter, he embarked on a fresh series of microscopical investigations little suspecting where they would lead.

'My attention,' he writes, 'was attracted by frequent complaints in the newspapers of the bad quality of the ground coffee sold and the many doubts expressed as to its genuineness.'

He turned his microscope on to sections of the whole coffee berry unroasted and roasted, of the roasted berry after it was ground and raw and roasted chicory root. 'Roasting and partial charring and blackening by no means destroyed the beautiful and minute structures and tissues entering into the composition of the coffee berry and chicory root. This being so, I knew that I had found the key to the detection of a variety of adulterations and admixtures of vegetable substances possessing organisation visible under the microscope.'

The Government met the vociferous complaints by appointing a Commission. A report was issued, and in answer to questions in the House, the Chancellor of the Exchequer replied, 'I hold in my hand the report of three of the most distinguished chemists of the day who state that neither by chemistry nor in any other way can the admixture of coffee with chicory be detected.'

Hassall promptly took up the challenge. The Chancellor made his statement in May, and on Friday 2 August 1850, Hassall read a paper *On the Adulteration of Coffee* before the Botanical Society of London. In so many words, he stated explicitly that 'nothing was more simple and certain than the detection of the admixture in question by means of the microscope.'

He records in his autobiography that he had already sent an abstract of this communication to Mr Dennes, Secretary to the Society: 'Nearly all the samples of roasted coffee I had bought at different shops were adulterated most extensively in a variety of ways, some consisted of little else than chicory . . . in many cases roasted wheat, peas, etc. were detected in considerable amounts . . . These spurious admixtures were sold under the most grandiloquent names and with statements absolutely false.' Mr Dennes sent a notice of the communication to the Press, which provoked some leading articles, e.g. in *The Times*, Monday 5 August 1850.

Mr Thomas Wakley had been exercised for years by the scandal of food adulteration. Friedrich Christian Accum had published in 1820 a *Treatise on Adulterations of Food and Culinary Poisons*, commonly referred to as 'Death in the Pot' from the quotation in the preface from 2 Kings IV, 40 'There is death in the pot.' John Dingwall Williams followed in 1830 with *Slow Poisoning or Disease and Death in the Pot and the Bottle* and in the following year the *Lancet* published an article on *Poisonous Confectionery* giving the results of some analyses made by William (later Sir William) Brooks O'Shaughnessy, M.D. at

Wakley's request. He sent for Hassall, as Hassall tells us, and said:

'I have observed what you have been doing, but you will never effect any lasting good until you are able to provide the names and the addresses of the parties of whom the articles were purchased, giving the results of the examination in all cases whether good or bad. Do you think it would be possible to do this without an amount of risk which might be ruinous?'

'I replied, yes, I believe it might be done. Of course the utmost care, caution and scrupulous exactitude would be necessary.' Then Mr Wakley asked me to put my views in writing and to draw up a definite and working scheme.

A few days later, on 13 August 1850, it was agreed, as the result of communication between Wakley and Hassall, that the latter should prepare a series of articles embodying the results of analyses of samples of food, beverages and drugs, of all kinds, to be purchased at various shops in and around London; these articles to be styled the *Reports of the Lancet Analytical Sanitary Commission* (a name proposed by Wakley) and to appear periodically and frequently, and to include the names and addresses of vendors of adulterated samples, the editor of the *Lancet* bearing all expense and legal responsibility. On 14 December 1853, a further agreement was signed, giving Hassall the sole right of separately publishing these reports from 1 January 1851 to 31 December 1854, in his own name, as Chief Analyst to the Commission, and under the title of *Food and its Adulterations*.[6]

The scheme on which the examinations were made was worked out jointly by Wakley and Hassall and Sir William O'Shaughnessy; they formed the *Lancet*'s Analytical and Sanitary Commission.

Wakley announced at the commencement of the enquiry:

'We have undertaken a task large enough to engage the attention of the Government of this country. With the exception of officers to observe and report upon diseased meat or fish, the public authorities take no cognisance of the adulteration and poisoning by the slower but equally sure mode of adulteration of food and drinks. We will bring the microscope and test tube to bear with unerring truth upon things hidden and secret enough to the unaided senses . . . for the protection of the public, the advantage of the fair trader, and the ultimate exposure and punishment of the fraudulent one.'[7]

The first the public learnt of the fresh chapter opening in Public Health was a special announcement in the *Lancet*.

THE ANALYTICAL SANITARY COMMISSION

Records of the Results of Microscopical and Chemical Analysis of the Solids and Fluids consumed by all Classes of the Public.

'Forewarned, Forearmed'

'Uncontaminated air and pure water are now universally regarded as necessary to the maintenance of healthy existence, and to obtain them we have appointed Boards of Health and Commissions of Sewers.

'We propose, then, for the public benefit to institute an extensive and somewhat vigorous series of investigations into the present condition of the various articles of diet supplied to the inhabitants of this great metropolis and its vicinity, and probably the inquiries will be extended to some of our distant cities and towns. Our special feature of these inquiries will be that they are all based upon actual observation and experiment; the microscope and the test tube throughout these investigations will be our constant companions. We shall borrow but little from the writings of others, preferring to labour and think for ourselves and to work out our conclusions in an independent manner.

'A second feature will consist in the introduction of faithful engravings illustrating all the more important points and particulars of each article.

'A third and highly important feature will be the *publication* of the *names* and *addresses* of the parties from whom the different articles, the analyses of which will be detailed, were purchased; the advantages of such a course of proceeding require no explanation.'[7]

Reports followed in the *Lancet* every week for a long time, and then fortnightly, during the years 1851–52–53–54. The first report on 4 January 1851 dealt with coffee; of 34 samples examined, all but three were adulterated with chicory, bean flour, potato flour; at a second examination on 20 August, 20 samples were all found adulterated. Sugar next received attention; 35 out of 36 examples swarmed with *Acari*, sugar mites, thus disclosing the cause of the prevalent 'Grocer's Itch'. Arrowroot was commonly found to be adulterated; Pepper, 'over half the samples adulterated', Water was examined from the point of metallic poisoning, e.g. by lead; Bread, 24 samples were all adulterated by alum; 14 out of 26 samples of milk had had water added, the yellow vegetable dye annatto being freely used to restore the natural tint; in turn an extensive range of food and liquids came under intense scrutiny.

'The exact mode of proceeding adopted in the case of each Report,' Hassall tells us, 'was as follows: selecting some suitable locality Mr Miller and I used to sally out from time to time, usually in the evening, often on Saturday nights, in all weathers and at all seasons of the year; we were provided with a bag to receive samples, paper and ink. Sometimes we entered the shop together, but more often I told Mr Miller what to buy and he made the actual purchase, while I was watching closely all that took place, so that I might be, if needed, a competent witness. On leaving the shop, the name of the vendor, the date and cost of the purchase, together with our initials, were at once inscribed in ink on the wrappers of the packages and it was the fixed rule, that no second purchase should ever be made until all these formalities had been carried out . . .

'The next morning, the samples were duly arranged and classified and their examinations commenced, a series of samples of the same article being taken for each report. But before any satisfactory examination of the sample could be made, it was necessary that the structure and microscopical characters of the vegetable substances themselves in their pure state, both as a whole and when ground and reduced to powder, should be studied and delineated; that they should be submitted if necessary to chemical analysis and that the probable adulterants of each article should be in succession subjected to similar scrutiny and analysis. Thus it was, that the foundation was laid, on which the determination of the question of the purity or otherwise of the articles to be reported upon, could be safely and surely based.

'The composition of the series of samples having now been

determined, the illustrative figures drawn by the aid of the camera lucida, and the wood engravings prepared, the next and final proceeding was to write the report.'

In this manner, during the four years the *Lancet* published reports, 'upwards of 2500 samples of food were examined and reported upon, with, in all cases, the names and addresses of the vendors, retail and wholesale. The reports embraced all the principal articles of consumption, both solids and liquids.'

The regulations for the M.B. London had required a certificate that the candidate had attended 'A Course of Practical Chemistry, comprehending Practical Exercises in conducting the more important processes of General and Pharmaceutical Chemistry; in applying tests for discovering the Adulteration of articles of the Materia Medica and the presence and nature of Poisons.' Hassall therefore had the subject fresh in mind, and was able to apply straightforward chemical tests where these were called for. But 'it was to the microscope, that the success of these investigations was due; but for this novel application of that instrument, the multitudinous adulterations practised on nearly every article of consumption could never have been discovered and exposed.'

John Thomas Queckett (who lectured on histology and catalogued the histological series at the Royal College of Surgeons) in 1850 proposed its employment as a means of discovering frauds; but there was as yet no systematized observation and scientific description of the minute structure of foodstuffs, nor any attempt at a general application of the instrument in the analysis of food and drugs.[6]

'The general result of these enquiries and investigations,' writes Hassall, 'showed that the adulteration of articles of consumption had been reduced to a system, to an art, and almost to a science; that it was universally practised; that adulteration was the rule and purity the exception, that everything that could be cheapened by admixture was so and that the articles thus debased were sold as genuine and often under the most high-flown names and with assertions of unblushing falsehood ... when we consider that many of the articles reported upon, as tea, coffee, cocoa, wines, spirits, tobacco, etc. were excisable, and that from the duties levied thereupon a large revenue was derived, and that a special scientific Board was in existence for the detection of their adulteration, furnished with a laboratory provided with microscopes and every needful requirement, it is indeed extraordinary that the state of things described should so long have been permitted to exist. The sums which were lost to the Revenue in past years must have been enormous . . . in excuse it may be urged that it was no part of the duty of (chemists) attached to the Board to ascertain whether non-excisable articles were pure or not . . . nor to determine whether any adulterations they detected were injurious to health.'

Wholesale adulteration, therefore, lethal on occasion, was the rule not the exception, and matters were not at all helped by the lazy views of some pharmacists and analytical chemists regarding certain admixtures. Professor Redwood of the Pharmaceutical Society of Great Britain denied at one meeting of the Society at which Hassall was present that annatto, the yellow vegetable dye commonly used to colour milk, cheese, etc. was adulterated. Whereupon at a subsequent (and crowded!) meeting Hassall produced conclusive evidence that it was grossly adulterated.

Chemical analysis revealed that poisonous compounds of arsenic, copper, mercury and lead were freely used to colour confectionery. There was copper in pickles, bottled fruits and vegetables; Venetian *Red* (ferric oxide), Armenian Bole (a red clay), and lead in potted meat and fish; sulphuric acid in brandy and gin.

In September 1855 Hassall read a paper at the Glasgow meeting of the British Association *On the Chemistry of the Adulteration of Food* which appears to have ended, rather inexplicably, in a wrangle about soil fertility between Liebig and Dr Gilbert, where 'the practical agriculturist carried off the honours of the day.'

In January Hassall read the paper mentioned above, to the Pharmaceutical Society, on *The Adulteration of Annatto* and casting his net further afield, reported next upon *The Bread of Edinburgh* and *The Oatmeal of Edinburgh*. They proved unexpectedly pure; Clayton regards this as evidence that the leaven of the *Lancet* reports was beginning to work.[6]

Hassall did not confine his attentions to food and drinks. He extended them to drugs. Opium, scammony, julep and rhubarb are some of those on which reports were published. Some reports appeared in the *Lancet*, others were published in two editions of *Adulterations detected in Food and Medicine* that appeared in 1857 and 1861.

In the complicated analysis of tobacco, snuff, and opium Hassall consulted and employed Dr Letheby, a well-known chemist of the day. On only one occasion did he find it necessary to consult a microscopist. A threatened action went so far as delivery of a declaration, and he therefore sent portions of the disputed sample to Mr Bowerbank and Mr Edward Quickette (Queckett?) 'for the purpose of corroboration and without giving any particulars.' In both cases he received 'confirmatory testimony' which would have been forthcoming had the case come to court.

He and Wakley of course were running grave risks in their protection of the public. 'The risk to Mr Wakley as proprietor of the *Lancet* was very great; there was the serious risk of being involved in grave litigation and possibly of heavy, if not ruinous, costs; for my part I risked all I possessed; namely my scientific and professional reputation.' The publication of articles giving vendor's names and addresses did lead to a few lawyer's letters being received, but only in the case above was a declaration delivered that Court proceedings were under consideration. Fear of what else might come out in Court alone stopped a great many actions from being brought, it may be assumed.

The *Lancet* reports were commented upon and discussed as they appeared in most scientific journals, and in the popular Press. If only a small number had been issued, they would have been a nine-days' wonder and then become, if not forgotten, yesterday's headlines, like Accum's *Death in the Pot*, or O'Shaughnessy's analyses of confectionery. When, however, they continued remorselessly 'weekly for a long time and then fortnightly', their impact was overwhelming.

The happiest comment was made by the *Quarterly Review*. Hassall, availing himself of the second agreement made with Wakley, re-issued the reports under his own name as '*Food and its Adulterations*', published in 1855. In respect of an article in this work, the *Quarterly Review* observed:

'A gun suddenly fired into a rookery could not cause greater commotion than did this publication of the names of dishonest tradesmen, nor does the daylight, when you lift a stone, startle ugly and loathsome things more quickly than the pencil of light streaming through a quarter-inch lens, surprised in their native ugliness the thousand and one illegal substances which enter more or less into every article of food which it will pay to adulterate. Nay, to such a pitch of refinement has the art of fabrication of alimentary substances reached, that the very articles used to adulterate are themselves adulterated; and while one tradesman is picking the pockets of his customers, a still more cunning rogue is, unknown to himself, deep in his own.'[8]

The pencil of light streaming through the lens might fancifully be called in modern parlance the 'laser beam' with which, not only in respect of food adulteration, Hassall cut through the metaphorical fog in which he worked.

Ultimately the reports led to a meeting convened on 11 December 1854 by Mr J. Postage, F.R.C.S., of Birmingham, urging the attention of the Legislature to the subject of the adulteration of food. The next step was the appointment on 16 June 1855 of a Parliamentary Select Committee under the presidency of Mr W. Scholefield, M.P. for Birmingham, before which Hassall was the chief scientific witness. The third step was the passing of the first general Adulteration Act, of 6 August 1860: 'An Act for Preventing the Adulteration of Articles of Food or Drink.'*

Hassall could not avoid treading on a great many toes, and in some quarters aroused a storm of abuse and criticism, not only from angry tradesmen as would be expected, but from scientists who noted the immense sensation the reports had caused and rushed to publish claims of priority.

Dr Letheby was prominent among these; Hassall disposed of his claims by producing the original letters and account which had closed his services, but Letheby took his revenge years later; it is noteworthy, says Clayton, that from beginning to end of the article *Adulteration* in the *Encyclopedia Britannica*, ninth edition 1875, written by Letheby, there is not one mention of Dr

---

* See note at end of chapter.

Hassall's name. 'There is, however, a reference to Dr Letheby himself.'[6]

Attempts by Hassall's critics failed to exploit a temporary coolness that arose between him and Wakley from the attention that Hassall received.

'It was,' says Spriggs, 'the most useful agitation in favour of legislative reform that ever engaged his (Wakley's) attention,[7] and, Hassall remarks, 'that Mr Wakley felt some disappointment is not surprising. He rightly thought his part in the publication of the reports should have received some public recognition.' The cloud soon blew over, and the former friendship was resumed as cordially as ever until Wakley left for Madeira. Hassall continued to contribute to the *Lancet* for another thirty years, and was on such good terms with Dr James Wakley, who succeeded his father as Editor, that James wrote a special article in 1881 defending the part Hassall played in the passing of the first Adulteration Act.

A silver statuette was presented to Hassall on 4 May 1856 in appreciation of his public services, at a public dinner held at the Freemasons Tavern presided over by Lord William Lennox in the absence of Viscount Ebrington, M.P.

A circular had been issued in 1855, announcing that a Committee was to be formed for the purpose of raising a Public Testimonial to Dr Arthur Hill Hassall in recognition of his labours in the preservation of Public Health.

'The grounds upon which this claim is founded are PURITY OR IMPURITY OF WATER. To Dr Hassall is due the honour of making the microscope subservient to the analysis of "organic matter". He was thus enabled to establish principles adopted to a considerable extent in the new Metropolis Water Bill.

'Laying bare the health-destroying and fraudulent ADULTERATION OF FOOD AND DRUGS; the great importance of the subject has been recognised by Parliament, and this mainly through the labours of Dr Hassall.'

The names of Edwin Chadwick and Dr Southwood Smith appear among the ninety-nine members of the Committee, also of Jabez Hogg, M.D., author of the book on the microscope mentioned earlier, and of John Coppin, M.A., and Richard Hassall M.D., too. Among others not in the Committee who expressed approval of the proposed testimonial to which they subscribed the eye is caught by the name of John Simon, F.R.S., the first Medical Officer of Health for the City of London. The name of Andrew Ross does not appear, but he was certainly present at the dinner as Hassall's guest.

At the presentation dinner, the Chairman proposed the health of Dr Hassall 'who gracefully acknowledged his gratitude at this public recognition of his work' and in reply praised the courage of Mr Wakley, whose health he proposed. Mr Wakley replying said, 'It was true there had been a difference between him and Dr Hassall but' – turning and bowing to the ladies on the dais – 'it was a merely lover's quarrel and we are now greater friends than ever.'

'A very elegant statuette,' writes Hassall, 'a real work of art, weighing some 400 ounces, was presented to me. The figure represents the Angel Ithuriel . . . clad in armour, touching with his spear Satan, who having assumed the shape of a toad, sits close by the ear of Eve, tempting her. The subject is taken from Milton's *Paradise Lost* and the pedestal bears these words from the same source –

> Him thus intent Ithuriel with his spear
> Touched lightly; for no falsehood can endure
> Touch of celestial temper; but returns
> Of force to its own likeness; up he starts
> Discovered and surprised.'

The Press reported that the testimonial 'is an exquisite work of art designed from Milton's *Paradise Lost* by the Rev. G. M. Braune, M.A. It stands about 3 feet 6 inches in height and the figure is modelled and chased (by M. Feret) in a manner rarely equalled in this country. One of the panels of the pedestal is occupied with a basso-relievo, representing the microscope and the chemical apparatus employed in the discovery of adulteration, while another bears the following inscription:

To

ARTHUR HILL HASSALL, M.D., F.L.S.,
ANALYST OF THE LANCET SANITORY
COMMISSION, AND AUTHOR
OF THE REPORTS OF THAT
COMMISSION, ENTITLED "FOOD
AND ITS ADULTERATIONS,"

BY

MEMBERS OF BOTH THE HOUSES OF
PARLIAMENT, BY MEMBERS OF
THE LEARNED PROFESSIONS, AND BY
OTHERS CONNECTED
WITH SCIENCE, LITERATURE, AND COMMERCE,
IN RECOGNITION
OF EMINENT PUBLIC BENEFITS CONFERRED BY HIS RARE
SCIENTIFIC SKILL AND INDEFATIGABLE LABOUR IN THE
DETECTION AND EXPOSURE OF A PERNICIOUS AND SYSTEMATIC
ADULTERATION OF FOOD AND MEDICINE.

May 15, 1856

'The symbolism of the design will be readily perceived. The Spirit of Good, as represented by the angel, is employing Science, symbolized by the spear, for the discovery of Truth, under the talismanic touch of which the fraud and falsehood of Adulteration, in the semblance of a toad, spring to light.'

(Two reports of the inscription, including that above, refer to the Sanatory Commission, presumably a misprint for Sanitary.)

The statuette is seen in the portrait of Hassall seated by his Ross microscope. Most appropriately so, for the one brought the other into existence, and perhaps this was in Hassall's mind when he posed for the picture. Without the microscope, without the 'laser beam' of light streaming through the lens, no public health services would have merited the award of the statuette. It is illustrated in Clayton's *Memoir*,[6] published in 1908, fifteen years after Hassall died. Mrs Hassall was then in Italy, and it was therefore presumably in Clayton's possession as Hassall's close friend and executor of his will. What has happened to it since? This avowedly exquisite work of art, three and a half feet high, containing 400 ounces of silver, that a museum would prize for its intrinsic value, other associations apart. Is it still in existence?

Food Adulteration Legislation

The First Act of 6 August 1860 was followed by that of 1872 responsible for the appointment of public analysts for the various counties and boroughs. In 1874 a Commission before which Hassall gave evidence was appointed to enquire into the working of the Act of 1872. The Food and Drugs Act of 1875 was based upon its report.

All subsequent legislation during the century that has since elapsed stems directly from the first Act of 1860 for which Hassall was directly responsible.

He published on the subject *Food and its Adulterations* 1855, a reprint of the *Lancet* reports; *Adulterations Detected* 1857, second edition 1861; and in 1876 *Food its Adulterations and the Methods for their Detection*.

An obituary in the *Analyst* observes: 'It is mainly in connection with the adulteration of food that Dr Hassall's claim to public recognition rests . . . In (his) death which occurred at San Remo, there has been removed from our midst one to whom the public and all Public Analysts owe a debt of gratitude.'[9]

References for Chapter Eight
1 Librarian, London University Library.
2 Librarian, London University Library.
3 E. P. Thomson, Eileen Yea, *The Unknown Mayhew*, Merlin Press 1971.
4 *Illustrated London News*, 10 October 1849, quoted by Priscilla Metcalfe in *Victorian London*, Cassell 1972.
5 Norman Longmate, *Alive and Well*, Penguin Books 1970.
6 E. G. Clayton, *A Memoir of the late Doctor Arthur Hill Hassall*, Baillière Tindall & Cox, 1908.
7 S. S. Sprigge, *The Life and Times of Thomas Wakley*, Longmans Green, 1897.
8 *Quarterly Review*, March 1855.
9 *The Analyst*, May 1894.

NINE

Cholera Fact and Fiction

Those who attended the dinner at the Freemasons Tavern had survived another cholera visitation two years previously. Cholera flared up in 1853, and assumed epidemic proportions the following year. Dr Snow described the outbreak in Soho 'as the most terrible outbreak which ever occurred in this kingdom.' In two days 197 people died, and in another week, in an area of only 250 yards long, there were more than 500 deaths.[1]

Nothing more clearly illustrates the metaphorical fog in which the doctors groped than what they wrote about cholera, which we may read in Protheroe Smith's *Tracts on the Cholera*.[2]

'Thus we have successive states; the one resulting from the other and producing a concatenation of symptoms, which have their origin in derangement of the *primae viae*.'

'Of the ultimate cause or first principle, from which Cholera results, I shall not attempt to offer any other solution than that it depends and is consequent on the will of the Great Author of Nature.'

John George French, M.R.C.S., formerly surgeon to St James's Cholera Hospital, believed the disease consisted essentially in paralysis of the heart; Professor Delpech, that it was an affection of the semilunar ganglion. George Gregory, M.D., Physician to the Smallpox Hospital, suspected that Morbific Germs were the cause, although they were anything but specific, and could cause almost any disease you cared to name given the right atmospheric conditions. Fish, fruit, atmospheric influence (including mysterious *cholera clouds*, one of which was held responsible for the appearance of the disease in Newcastle on Tyne) each were set forth as the exciting cause. It was even suggested that the flinty frustules of diatoms might be responsible. I have known water fowl to be killed by an acute enteritis caused by their abrasive action, like that of powdered glass, when packed among confervoid algae the birds swallowed. But ducks are not human beings.

Dr John Snow produced very good evidence that cholera was water-borne by his famous map, which showed how thickly fatal cases clustered round a pump in Broad Street, St James's. In almost every house which had used water from the pump the disease had appeared. He originally established that the mortality rate, quoted in the last chapter, was higher among those receiving water from the Vauxhall and Southwark Company, which still drew water from the Thames, than in those supplied by the Lambeth Company which had moved to Teddington. William Budd had shown in the previous year, when dealing with an outbreak of water-borne typhoid, not cholera, at Kingswood, that it was not sewage but sewage plus excreta from fever patients that caused the disease. Richard Hassall, M.D., in his tract on the Cholera[3] wisely eschewed first causes, gave fair notice it might be water-borne, and concentrated on methods of sanitary control proved to be of practical value, against the possibility – or probability – of another outbreak.

Dr Snow died in 1858, and eight years later, in 1886, the last great cholera epidemic (though not the last outbreak) in the British Isles 'provided conclusive proof of his theory, when 7,000 people in the East End of London died of cholera in a few weeks, after a new employee at a waterworks had allowed unfiltered water, containing sewage from a house where cholera was present, to enter the main water supply.'[1]

The Board of Health was greatly alarmed by Hassall's exposure of the quality of the Metropolitan water, and had it learnt that cholera could be contracted from the filthy liquid, it was no more than would be expected. However, the Board was dissolved on 1 July 1854, and Snow's report did not appear until 1855, when it attracted little attention; indeed, he was accused of impeding progress, if water could be blamed for cholera, why bother to clean up the streets? Hassall's crushing indictment of the Metropolitan water supply had been made three or four years earlier, in 1850, and had the authorities acted more vigorously on his evidence, and made the Water Companies move upstream within three, not five years, Snow might well have lacked such conclusive testimony of comparative mortality rates.

After the original Board of Health established by the Public Health Bill of 10 February 1848, with a life of five years, had been wound up, Chadwick and Dr Southwood Smith retired into private life. A modified Board of Health functioned to a limited extent from 31 August 1854, under Sir Benjamin Hall, until 1858, when its functions were taken over by the Privy Council. (Sir John Simon asked the Council in 1863 to look into the appalling conditions in hospitals which prompted Christopher Heath to warn his readers of the risks to health run by those working in them.)

When the cholera broke out once more, Hassall was promptly recruited as the recognised authority on all that related to water.

'Shortly after the outbreak of cholera in London in 1854,' he writes, 'Sir Benjamin Hall having just been made President of the General Board of Health by Lord Palmerston, I was appointed one of the Medical Inspectors under the Board, and I had two extensive districts to supervise, Lambeth Parish and Wandsworth Union; these had to be visited and written reports sent in daily, and an amount of work was entailed which was both harassing and exhausting. The experience thus gained of the various insanitary conditions and surroundings under which the people in the poorer and denser districts lived, proved afterwards of much practical value to me. The particulars of these inspections will be found recorded in the official reports of the Board at that time. That there should be sudden visitations of infectious diseases after the experience I had gained, no longer occasioned me surprise.

'Sir Benjamin Hall was a most efficient and energetic President; he quickly formed a Medical Council to advise and assist him, consisting of some of the foremost authorities of the day. A Scientific Committee of Investigation was also appointed; this consisted of Mr Glaisher for the Meteorological, Dr R. D. Thomson for the Chemical, and myself for the Microscopical portions of the work. My investigations embraced the examination of drinking water; the rice water discharges of cholera; the blood; renal excretion, and the clothes of cholera patients. Upon each of these subjects separate reports were prepared and afterwards published by order of the Houses of Parliament, together with all the other documents having reference to this Cholera visitation.

'The Microscopical investigation relative to water was very extensive and minute; it embraced the water of all the Companies, taken from the mains and also from houses in which cholera was actually present, or in which deaths had very recently taken place; water from shallow wells, in some cases those supplying cholera-stricken houses; from Artesian and other deep wells; water from the chalk both before and after it had been softened. This report was largely illustrated by a number of beautifully drawn figures. The drawings were made by my own artist, Mr Henry Miller, lithographed by Mr Tuffen West and were coloured by hand. I have not to this day seen delineations of the organic matters, dead and living, contained in waters used for drinking purposes equal to these for fidelity and excellence.

'Abundant evidence was produced of mischief arising from the intermittent system of supply and of the polluting effects of the storage of water in cisterns, butts, tubs, pans, jugs, etc. In many cases the cisterns had no lids and in others these were fastened down, so that the cisterns could not be cleansed.

'The results were for the most part confirmatory of those previously arrived at by me and which it is not necessary to state again in detail. Of the fact of the occasional admixture of the water of the Thames in its course between the Metropolitan bridges with the water of the sea, further proofs were given.

'The microscopical examination of the rice water discharges of cholera furnished interesting evidence which was really of much more importance than was at first supposed. In order that no time should be lost before the examinations were made, my microscope was placed in readiness in the Abernethy Ward of St Bartholomew's Hospital. The autopsies necessary were made by myself in the Wandsworth Mortuary. From my report on this subject I will now extract certain passages, relative to the presence in the rice water discharges of *Vibriones*, or as they would now be termed *Bacilli*.

'Myriads of Vibriones were detected in every drop of each sample of the rice water discharge hitherto subjected to examination; of these Vibriones some formed short threads more or less twisted while others were aggregated into masses which presented a dotted appearance. See Figure 26.* From observations which have been elsewhere recorded,† it appears that two of the circumstances necessary to the development of vibriones are a feebly acid or more usually *an alkaline fluid* and organic matter, especially animal, in a state of decomposition, more or less advanced. Now in the rice water discharges of cholera both of these conditions are fulfilled. We have next to enquire what is the origin or source of these vibriones and what is their relation to cholera? It is possible that they may obtain entrance into the stomach and bowels by means of the atmosphere, but it is perfectly certain that they do frequently gain admission through some of the impure waters consumed in which I have not infrequently detected the presence of vibriones, sometimes in considerable numbers. Once introduced into the alimentary canal they are brought into contact with conditions highly favourable to their development and propagation, both of which take place with extraordinary rapidity. I made for the sake of comparison some examinations of healthy evacuations. I found only a small number of vibriones and these not in all cases and when present they occurred in the lower part of the intestinal canal, where in healthy digestion incipient decomposition first takes place. In cholera cases the vibriones are met with as high up as the duodenum.

'Without however at all supposing that there is an essential or primary connection between these vibriones and cholera, their occurrence in such vast numbers in the rice water discharges of that disease is not without interest and possibly is of importance; thus their presence seems to indicate that the fluid thrown out into the intestinal canal in cholera and especially into the small intestines, is in a state more than ordinarily prone

---

* In this figure are shown the short, straight, single bacillus with slightly enlarged ends; the twisted bacillus, on which Koch has bestowed the distinctive but somewhat fanciful name of the 'comma' bacillus, the union of two or more bacilli and the occasional extension of these into a more or less twisted thread, indicating the relation of this bacillus to a species of *Spirillum* very similar to that found by me many years since in the waters of the Serpentine, to which reference has already been made, and lastly, the colonies of bacilli.

† Transactions of the Medico-Chirurgical Society 1853.

to pass into decomposition and that the fluid itself is more than usually alkaline. A condition of undue alkalinity would assuredly act as a source of irritation to the mucous membrane of the intestines as alkaline urine does to that of the bladder.

'The existence of these vibriones in the evacuations may also possibly explain in some degree the success of sulphuric acid in checking the diarrhoea. Thus, that acid when freely administered destroys the conditions essential to the development of the vibriones and so destroys the vibriones themselves.'

Hassall continues: 'These vibriones, as was to be expected, were also found on the clothes in many cases and in reference to this point the following remark occurs in my report on the *Skin and Clothes* of cholera patients: "If these vibriones possess any influence on the production of cholera, or if the rice water discharges contain any substance or principle capable of producing that disease, we can readily understand how the cleansing of the clothes might in some cases give rise to cholera in those engaged in washing them."

'Professor Koch has stated, that in nearly half the cases of cholera dejecta submitted to him, a rapid microscopical examination has enabled him to detect the presence of the cholera bacillus and to set at rest any doubt which might be otherwise entertained as to the nature of the case. He was thus often enabled to declare with the utmost promptitude, even by telegraph, whether the discharges forwarded to him contained the cholera bacillus and really represented cases of cholera or not. Had those examinations taken place under the specially favourable conditions in which mine were made, the presence of the bacilli would doubtless have been discovered in most cases, my observations having been made on the dejecta, usually quite free from all contamination, of patients actually at the moment in the full stage of the disease.

'In my examinations the microscope was placed in a hospital ward filled with cholera patients, I was thus able to obtain the rice water discharge in its purest state and to submit it to immediate scrutiny. Some of the bacilli seen no doubt belonged to more than one species, but from the characters exhibited and which are fairly represented in the figure above referred to and from their general agreement with Koch's description, there is not the smallest doubt that the cholera bacillus was present in the discharges in nearly every case and was first seen by me during the Cholera epidemic of 1854, now nearly 40 years since.'

There can be no doubt that Hassall did indeed see the cholera vibriones as he claims. They would be present virtually in pure culture in the stools he examined.

A modern authority[4] points out that it is easy to mistake ordinary water bacteria for the cholera organism. They confused the issue in Koch's day. Hassall however is not deceived: 'In impure waters . . . I have not infrequently detected the presence of vibriones, sometimes in considerable numbers.' They were not likely to be those of cholera, for it does not survive long in nature; and they were rare in the normal stools of patients who presumably had drunk the same impure water. Bacteria were no novelties. Ehrenberg figures them in his *Die Infusionthierchen*, they appear in Pritchard's *Natural History of Animalcules* (1835) and from long experience Hassall would be familiar with the common water bacteria visible under his high-power objective.

'In healthy evacuations,' he writes, 'I found only a small number of vibriones and those not in all cases, and when present they occurred in the lower part of the intestinal canal . . . in cholera cases the vibriones are met with as high up as the duodenum.'

As to their significance, in cholera patients, whatever he may have suspected he wisely contented himself by observing, 'Without supposing there is a connection between these vibriones and cholera, their occurrence in such vast numbers is not without significance and *possibly is of importance.*'*

He drew attention to them in his reports to the Board and warned that they might be responsible for cholera among those who washed contaminated clothes. More he could not say in the medical climate of his day and in the absence of further proof. A first step meant isolation of the organism in pure culture, beyond the technique of those times in the strict sense that bacteriology demands. Had the question of pure cultures attracted Hassall's attention, it has been suggested, in discussing his studies of fungal disease, that he might have succeeded

---

* Present writer's italics.

sufficiently to anticipate Koch in more than one particular.

Numerous cases have occurred in man of accidental laboratory infection from cholera cultures, some of them fatal,[4] and
Hassall innocently ran the most hideous risks, dabbling in fresh
rice water stools, without rubber gloves, to make wet-mount
preparations for the microscope, conducting solitary post-
mortems to the endless jangling of church bells in the reeking
candle-lit Wandsworth mortuary, whence all but he had fled,
so great was the terror the cholera inspired.

His report, dated 21 December 1854, 'containing the results
of the Microscopical Examination of different Waters, principally those used in the Metropolis' illustrated by twenty-five
coloured plates 'the drawings made by my own artist Mr
Miller, lithographed by Mr Tuffen West, and coloured by
hand' was ordered by the Queen to be laid before both Houses
of Parliament, as mentioned in the last chapter.

Reports on the result of Microscopical Examination of Rice
Water Evacuations (December 1854) the Urine, the Blood and
the Skin of Cholera Patients (January 1855) also of the Air
Respired and Clothes Worn (22 January 1855) illustrated by
figures are included in the Appendix of the above Report.
(General Board of Health. Reports of Commissioners 1854–55.
XXI.)

The Board was groping desperately in the metaphorical fog
for any facts that might ward off future outbreaks of the
horrifying plague that struck without warning and killed within
hours. Across the road from York Railway Station the graves of
cholera victims bear witness that it was by no means confined to
London. In that fatal year 1854 there were 20,000 deaths from
cholera in England. Nor had the Health of Towns Commission,
which thoroughly investigated fifty English towns in 1846–7,
found that the City had any prerogative of squalor.

For Hassall, it was High Noon, those Victorian middle 'fifties
to early 'sixties. A recognised and established authority, he met
on an equal footing 'a noted and earnest band of sanitary
reformers; I was a contemporary of Sutherland, Southwood,
Smith, Farr, Milroy, Simon, Thomson, Glaisher, Parkes and
though last not least Edwin Chadwick. I was officially associated with most of them in official enquiries' and, he adds
modestly, 'I may fairly claim to have been one of the earliest

sanitary reformers in England.' After Kingsley had published *The Water Babies*, in which he is mentioned, Hassall's name became a household word, as likely to be heard in the nursery as downstairs in the parlour among the grown-ups discussing his exposures of polluted water and adulterated food.

Not surprisingly he was consulted, as he notes, on a great variety of questions relating to the public health. 'I was therefore frequently called upon to give evidence in trials in law courts, chiefly for the plaintiffs, rarely for the defendants.'

In 1854 he moved from Park Street to No. 8 Bennett Street, St James's, and from there to 74 Wimpole Street, where he practised from 1857–67. He had an analytical laboratory fitted up at each new address, where he was assisted by a succession of young men, some of whom became famous. Among them were Dr A. H. Allen, later a distinguished President of the Society of Public Analysts, author of a work on analytical chemistry, Mr Otto Hehner, another President, an eminent expert in the chemistry of oils and fats, and W. D. Borland, who became an authority on the chemistry and technology of explosives.

Hassall himself was elected first Vice-President of the Society of Analytical Chemists, although he admits ruefully he was a very bad one in point of attendance. He retained an interest, even after he settled in San Remo, in the laboratory at 43 and 44 Holborn Viaduct. It was from there that E. G. Clayton wrote to W. Carruthers, F.R.S., at the British Museum (Natural History) about his collection of algae, some months after Hassall died. While he was at Wimpole Street Hassall spent time that might have been better employed in trying to produce a commercial flour of meat. He was also associated for a time with a factory producing purified food but the response from an ungrateful public was poor and it was given up.

He was now at least in receipt of regular income that freed him from pressing financial anxieties, having been appointed Second Medical Referee to the United Kingdom Life Assurance Company, in 1852, through the agency of Mr Hale Thompson, until it was merged in 1862 with the North British and Mercantile Insurance Company, which he served in the same capacity. 'The latter office on my retirement granted me a honorarium which I received for a long time.'

About the time he was appointed to the United Kingdom Company, he was also offered a Lectureship in Botany at St Thomas's Hospital, 'an offer which I declined, partly because I was much pressed with work of one kind and another, and in part, because I considered it would not have helped me in practice, which was of course the chief goal at which I was necessarily aiming. In this latter view I was possibly mistaken, as the Lectureship would probably have led to my being placed on the medical staff of the Hospital.'

However, a year later he was appointed as one of the physicians of the Royal Free Hospital, through the interest of Mr Wakley and Dr Alexander Marsden. 'It well deserved its name of "Free",' wrote Hassall, 'for its gates were open to every destitute and disabled person without the necessity of obtaining a letter of recommendation.' He was attached to the Hospital for many years, becoming ultimately the Senior Physician. 'I used to attend the medical out-patient department regularly twice a week,' he writes, 'seeing on each occasion a great many of the applicants and I had more beds at my disposal for inpatients than is usual in the case of the older hospitals, owing to the staff of that Hospital being less numerous. The field of practice and the opportunities for acquiring practice were thus very considerable.'

At one time efforts were made by the hospital authorities and medical staff to found a Medical School in connection with the hospital, and Hassall was allotted a Lectureship in the Practice of Medicine. The College of Surgeons however would not accept certificates for hospital attendance at the School because the number of beds occupied was insufficient, 'and thus the School came to an untimely end.' To commemorate his services, the Hospital has lately named a ward to his memory the Hassall Ward.

Concentrating on the urine, whose deposits gave scope to his microscope, he published in 1860 a work on Urinary Disorders which was quickly sold out and appeared in a much larger edition in 1863 under the title of *The Urine in Health and Disease*. 'This embraced over 400 pages of letterpress and 79 engravings many coloured by hand and drawn by Mr Miller with the aid of the Camera (lucida.)' Three interesting observations made by Hassall are, firstly, that in acid urine two fungi develop,

Penicillium glaucum if albumen, *Mycoderma cerevisae* if sugar, is present. 'The fungus test is thus valuable for the detection of very small quantities of sugar in urine which in some cases the ordinary tests fail to discover.' His observations on the presence of indigo in urine 'were not altogether new, for Prout many years before had detected it on one occasion only, while in 1850 Debuyne identified it in the urine of a dropsical patient.' But at the time Hassall encountered it, there was no appreciation of how commonly it occurred.

The Hassall's Corpuscles of Cystitis, already discussed, are his third contribution of importance, 'first described,' as he tells us, 'in my article on the fourth edition of Dr Bird's *Urinary Deposits* in the *Medico-Chirurgical Review* for July 1853.'

These orthodox professional activities were carried forward at the same time as his arduous exposures of the polluted Metropolitan water supply and the long series of reports on food adulteration in the *Lancet*. It was after strenuous days at the Hospital or the offices of the Insurance Company that he sallied out with Mr Miller to buy food samples. 'Now these nocturnal excursions,' he writes, 'brought us into many curious parts of London and gave us a wonderful insight into the habits and ways of life of the people in the poorer districts; in summer they were pleasant and interesting enough, but in winter most trying and wearisome, waiting and hanging about we became chilled to the bone, sometimes not arriving home till near midnight.' (Was Miller a member of Hassall's household?)

Add to all these activities his own private practice and it is clear he constantly taxed himself to the utmost, physically as well as mentally. It would not be surprising to hear of a long holiday, perhaps a sea-voyage, to recover from his exhaustion. Something more sinister struck him down in 1866.

'I had noticed for some time past that in the mornings I had a little cough. Leaving the *Lancet* offices one day, feeling much as usual, a loud ringing cough came on quite suddenly. I had experienced a similar fit of coughing a day or two before, and this time a little blood followed. This gave me a shock; I got into a cab and went home.' Haemorrhage continued at intervals for some hours 'when a friend in the house* without my knowledge

---

* Was it Mr Miller – if he was resident in the house?

sent for Sir George Burrows. He came at once, ordered me to bed, while preparing for this a profuse haemorrhage suddenly ensued.'

A very long illness followed. 'I was in the greatest danger,' he writes, 'and throughout it I was assiduously attended with the utmost kindness by Sir George Burrows and Sir Richard Quain. I have often thought and still think of their goodness in diverting so much of their valuable time to my case, and for which I have ever been grateful.'

References for Chapter Nine

1 Norman Longmate, *Alive and Well*, Penguin Books, 1970.
2 Protheroe Smith, *Tracts on the Cholera including the Cholera Gazette 11 February 1832*, and
3 Richard Hassall M.D., *Cholera its nature and Treatment*, Henry Renshaw, London 1854.
4 Wilson, G. S. & Miles, A. *Topley & Wilson's Principles of Bacteriology and Immunity*, 5th ed., London: Edward Arnold, 1966.

TEN

Ventnor and the Founding of the Hospital

'My right lung was damaged,' Hassall tells us 'by the pleurisy at Notting Hill. But little further trouble had up to this time resulted from this cause and under more favourable conditions of life and surroundings than those in which I was placed in London, probably never would have troubled me. My case turned out to be one of fibroid phthisis of the right lung, a form so graphically described by Sir Andrew Clark,– distinct in some essential particulars from ordinary phthisis; it is much more chronic and results in more or less destruction and contraction of the lung affected. So great and persistent is the contraction, that in some cases, as is in my own, the heart becomes displaced and is drawn over to the affected side. This displacement embarrasses and impedes the action of the heart often seriously. But the great distinction is the absence of the bacilli of true tubercle.

'Soon after my recovery, I attended a *conversazione* at the Royal College of Physicians. Sir George Burrows, who it will be remembered attended me throughout my illness, was President of the College and he and the Censors were receiving the guests as they arrived. On my presenting myself, Sir George exclaimed: "Why, Hassall, what business have you here? You know you ought to have been buried long ago; why were you not?"'

It is surprising, after E. G. Clayton records that Hassall had a slight, frail figure, although of course he only knew him after illness had dragged him down. Certainly Hassall possessed a resilience at once remarkable and enviable, but even so the road back to health was a weary one. When it was safe for him to be

---

* But surely first of all by Sir Dominic Corrigan – *fibroid phthisis not occurring in miners* – all those years ago in Dublin, when Sir Dominic attended him while he was ill with typhoid.

moved, he went to his brother at Richmond. 'I well remember
the journey there . . . the vehicle was a special kind; it bore a
close resemblance to a hearse, as I did not fail to notice, and as
in a hearse I was put in at the back, lying full length. The
journey although made under these circumstances interested
me . . . to be out again after so long confinement in bed.' He
made some progress at Richmond 'under my brother's care and
Dr Tweedie's medical advice,' but it was slow and at times
doubtful.

'I was taken to Hastings . . . but my bedroom was at the back
of the house built close under a cliff and it was so dark it had to
be lighted even in the day-time; it seemed like a vault or
sepulchre.' His expostulations brought a change to brighter
quarters at St Leonards: 'Here I was attended professionally
most ably and kindly by Dr Blakiston. For a long time it was a
struggle between life and death and it was very doubtful which
would prevail.'

Winter was coming on, there was snow on the ground, 'still
another change of climate was advised and I was removed to
Ventnor.' This was so obvious a choice it was a pity it was not
made earlier, although he might have been too weak at first
even for the short sea trip to the island.

One of the most beautiful spots in all England, Ventnor must
have seemed to the sick man an earthly paradise after the grime
and noise of London. Terraces of houses that still have a
Victorian and Edwardian flavour[1] ascend to St Boniface Down,
the highest point of the island. The great coastal terrace of the
Undercliff runs westwards for six miles to Blackgang Chine,
and eastwards to Bonchurch, just on the outskirts of Ventnor,
where A. C. Swinburne is buried. On the west end of the town
stands Steephill Castle in its beautiful grounds, built by John
Hamborough in 1833, who went blind before it was finished
and never saw the lovely house he[2] created. Two ill-fated
Queens stayed there while Hassall was resident in the town, the
Empress of Austria in 1874 and Empress Eugénie of France in
1877.[2] The Empress of Austria he was to come to know very
well.

Sheltered by the Downs from north winds, the warm climate
fosters a sub-tropical vegetation. 'On the whole it may be
said of this unique locality,' observes Hasall, 'that its climate is

scarcely to be equalled in Great Britain. If it were easily accessible from the mainland great would have been its prosperity and Bournemouth would never have surpassed it in this respect.' Hassall would have reached it by way of the ferry from Portsmouth to Ryde, and then by the railway on through Shanklin to his destination at the railway station in Ocean View Road.

Climbing the steep streets I was puzzled how Hassall got round them with only one good lung and a displaced heart. When he became a resident, he lived at St Catherine's House in Church Street, which runs uphill. 'He first appears at that address in Hill's *Directory of the Isle of Wight*, 1871. The last entry for him at that address appears in White's *Gazetteer and Directory of Hampshire and the Isle of Wight*, 1878. In the next *Directory* that for 1883, we find the house occupied by a Dr Sinclair Coghill, M.D.'[3] There could be no return to living in London. For some years he travelled to and fro twice a week to attend at the Insurance Offices, but he made his home in Ventnor.

'It was pointed out,' Hassall records, 'that I should never be fit for the climate of, or for professional life in London, and it was suggested that I should remain permanently in Ventnor. After some consideration I determined to adopt this suggestion and to make Ventnor the centre of my future work and new career. I therefore parted with the lease of my house and furniture in Wimpole Street to Dr Green, who has resided there ever since.'

In the year of his illness a Civil List Pension of £100 a year had been conferred on him by Lord Derby 'in consideration of his public services.' In the memorial, dated 28 August 1866, praying for a pension, these services were stated to have been, 'The Elucidation and Exposure of Adulteration in Food, Drink, and Medicine,' 'the gain to the Revenue by his labours, as also the gain to the Health of the Public,' and 'his attention to Sanitary Questions generally, especially the Water Supply and Cholera, the exposure of the former resulting in a new and improved Supply.'

He was pre-eminent in all matters relating to food and its purity, and once he had settled down, he tells us, 'I had a commodious laboratory built where original investigations were carried out and analyses made. I had two assistants, Mr

Arthur Angell and Mr Otto Hehner; both of these afterwards
became well-known names in chemistry and are public analysts
under the Act for the suppression of adulteration.'

Hassall had kept his name before the public by publishing
some letters in the *Lancet* and in the daily Press (e.g. the *Standard*
18 February 1864) on the dangers of illuminating oils with low
flash points. At the Ventnor laboratory his assistants now
proceeded to discover a method by which the adulteration of
butter with animal fats could be detected. However, he says, 'I
was entirely dependent on my profession,' and all that that now
earned him were his fees as Medical Referee to the Insurance
Company, having, as he tells us, 'relinquished my post of
physician at the Royal Free Hospital as well as my private
practice, in consequence of the serious illness which befell me in
1866.'

He had a salary from the Insurance Company, and his Civil
List Pension; there would be consultant's fees for opinions on
matters relating to food adulteration; and there would be
royalties from his books. It is difficult therefore to understand
how he met the costs of building and equipping a laboratory,
and found the salaries of two assistants to staff it. Possibly funds
were provided from the sale of his practice to Dr Green. It still
suggests pinching and scraping, and that he could never have
had the opportunity to put anything aside. The Victorian
status symbol of a fashionable medical man was a smart
turnout of a carriage and pair with a coachman. Did he hire the
best available rig when patients began to seek his services?
More expense would thereby be involved, in addition to the
cost of the bi-weekly journeys to London. 'The journeys were
very trying as they entailed much waiting about and exposure,
since the sea had to be crossed and there were several changes of
conveyances, cabs, tramcars and railways,' he tells us, yet for
financial reasons they could not be given up.

He must have been thankful to return to the peace and balmy
air of Ventnor after these trips into the London fogs. 'It soon
struck me as remarkable,' he wrote, 'that nothing had been
done in so highly favoured a district in the way of establishing a
hospital or sanatorium, especially a Hospital for the benefit of
our poorer brethren suffering from Diseases of the Lungs; it
seemed to me that it was just the place for such an institution, of

which indeed there was a great need. The Brompton Hospital for Consumption, though a valuable institution, in some respects did not, and still does not fulfil all the needful conditions of climate and surroundings. In fact,' he remarks with unconscious reflection upon his own earlier choice of domicile, 'the climate of London is most unsuitable for diseases of the lungs, it being damp and depressing, nearly sunless in the winter and the air carbon-laden and impure.' (There were no Smoke Abatement Acts in force then!) 'Certainly it cannot be said that the inmates of an institution thus situated are placed under the most favourable conditions for their recovery . . . The Curative Hospital for sufferers from Diseases of the Organs of respiration should be in some suitable spot in the country.'

He occupied his enforced leisure while travelling backwards and forwards 'in cab, tramcar, and railway' by planning such a hospital.

Villemin, and Cohnheim and Salomonson, had yet to demonstrate by their studies during the decade 1870–80 that tuberculosis was an infective disease. Nonetheless, Hassall decided that the institute he envisaged should be designed on the 'Separate System', 'that the patients should be separated, as far as practicable.'

In a striking passage, he throws light on the bad old system under which he had studied as a student and practised as a physician on a hospital staff, a system responsible for conditions Simon had asked the Privy Council to investigate.

'My experience had shown me the evils associated with the ward or aggregate system; the mixture of cases, medical and surgical, infectious and non-infectious, many suffering from wholly different diseases, some convalescing, some very ill, others perhaps dying; some noisy and boisterous and each being in sight or hearing of the others' sufferings. These evils,' he adds, writing in retirement, 'have no doubt been much mitigated since the period to which I refer, but there is still room for further improvement; the wards are now usually smaller and there is a better classification.'

Well might Dickens write, 'In our rambles through the streets of London after evening has set in, we often pause beneath the windows of some public hospital and picture to ourselves the gloomy and mournful scenes that are passing within.'[4]

Hassall's dreams of a hospital could never materialise without money. The first and all-essential step was to obtain funds. He therefore drew up a prospectus, setting out his proposals 'to build eight blocks of semi-detached houses; each house to accommodate six patients; each patient to have a separate bedroom facing south; two sitting rooms in each house to be used in common by the six patients. Eight houses were to be for men, eight for women, separated by a Chapel. The whole range of houses and chapel to be united by a subway along which a tramway would run. Spacious corridors and verandahs were to be a feature of each house, but each house was to be so far complete in itself that it could be registered as a separate or miniature hospital. To the extent of about one third or a little less the Hospital was to be self-supporting.'

The response of several charitable organisations to the prospectus was 'encouraging beyond expectation'. Mr Frederick Leaf, of the firm of Leaf and Co., Old Change, City, paid a personal visit. He and his wife became the first Life Governors, and the Leaf family's generosity was later commemorated by calling one of the blocks of houses by that name.

When about £1700 had been contributed, Lord Monson, acting for the Hon. E. C. A. Pelham, then a minor, leased a site on the west side of Ventnor but in the parish of St Lawrence; the site he suggested 'was so excellent in every way, so well sheltered and so beautiful that had I had the choice of the whole undercliff I could not have found a better.' A piece of glebe land attached to the church of St Lawrence was added by the Rector, the Rev. Charles Malden, who greatly favoured the project, 'making in all twenty-two acres of land secured at a very moderate rental on leases of nine hundred and ninety-nine years, as is the custom in the Isle of Wight.' The Rt. Hon. Sir Lawrence Peel, a retired Indian judge living at Ventnor, readily agreed to be Chairman of a Committee of Management formed from local residents, and the Governor of the Isle of Wight, the Rt. Hon. Lord Eversley, as readily consented to act as first President.

Two years after Hassall had arrived at Ventnor the first block was completed in 1868 and opened for patients; the architect was Mr Thomas Hellyer of Ryde 'who willingly filled the office without fee or reward.' Queen Victoria was prayed to lay the foundation stone of the second block of houses, completed in 1869. Although quite close at Osborne House, she was in semi-retirement, mourning the death of the Prince Consort on 15 December 1861. In announcing his death to the nation, she confessed herself 'the heartbroken Queen of England.' Her Royal Highness the Princess Louise therefore came as her representative. The morning of her visit was very wet, but suddenly the skies cleared and the sun came out. Driving from the station, the Princess was almost involved in an accident, for the postilions failed to check the horses on the steep slope. 'But for some bystanders the carriage might have been overset.'

'The laying of this stone,' writes Hassall, 'was one of the first public acts of the Princess, who was then quite young . . . to myself fell the duty of explaining all the details, of conducting Her Royal Highness over the grounds and of aiding in planting the inevitable royal trees.'

As the morning had been so wet, the gardeners had concluded there would be no planting of trees. 'The holes were dug,' but there were no trees and no gardeners. 'I exclaimed "This is really too bad, get some trees!" The people ran right and left and tore up all sorts of shrubs, two were selected and planting duly accomplished to the amusement of the Princess and the numerous visitors.'

In reply to an address presented by the President, the Rt. Hon. Viscount Eversley, the voice of the young Princess comes across the years: 'The Queen, my dear mother, on whose behalf I appear among you, feels a deep interest in this admirable charity and sympathises with the effort you are making to extend its benefits. It has ever been the desire of Her Majesty's heart (and every member of her family shares it) to promote every enterprise for the relief of her suffering subjects. The special diseases for which the Hospital is designed are those for which art can do least and nature most. May God therefore grant that the pure and health-giving climate of this beautiful district may be blessed to the restoration of all who shall be admitted to this noble institution.'

Hassall tells us, 'this touching reply has been duly printed, framed and hung up in the Hospital where it can be seen and read by all.'

Queen Victoria it is well known did take a warm, personal interest in her subjects' well being (witness her interviewing of Crimean veterans.) She became the Patroness of the Hospital and paid a personal visit years later on 11 February 1888, when Hassall unfortunately was far away at San Remo and not able to attend. Her family, and Royalty generally, took a great interest in the Hospital. 'The Empress of Austria, then resident at Steephill Castle, was patroness of a bazaar held in the grounds'; the Crown Prince and Princess of Prussia, afterwards the Emperor Frederick and Empress Victoria of Germany, paid a visit: 'the manner of the Crown Prince was so kind and gentle it was not easy to realise the fact that he had taken a leading and active part in the fierce strife of war,' presumably a reference to the Franco–Prussian War of 1870. The ninth block of houses was opened in 1887 by the Prince and Princess Henry of Battenberg, and Prince Leopold, Duke of Albany, was President of the Hospital at the time of his death.

The 'Special Principle' upon which the Hospital was founded – 'for those for whom art can do least and nature most' – attracted a great deal of notice. Professor von Schrötter of Vienna, Hassall tells us, sent his assistant to inspect the institution with the object 'of founding at the Professor's instance the first consumption hospital in the Austrian Empire at Vienna; Dr Pistor, Health Officer of Berlin, has also paid a visit to the Hospital, and he expressed himself in high terms as to its efficiency; again Dr Billet of the Military Hospital of St Omer has recently published a highly favourable article upon it, in *Le Journal d'Hygiène*; lastly it is proposed to erect at Killiney, near Dublin, a Hospital for Consumption on the same system, each patient being provided with a separate bedroom.'

In 1881 the hospital was visited by the British Medical Association, and in reference to this visit the *British Medical Journal* wrote: 'The Ventnor Hospital was much admired; no other Hospital in Europe can compare with it for the completeness with which the Cottage system is carried out and for the combination of comfort and scientific fitness for its peculiar purpose.'

The following year, 1882, Koch announced his discovery of

the tubercle bacillus, and, Hassall writes, 'the discovery of the tubercle bacillus has led to the adoption of a variety of precautions at the Hospital with a view to diminish the risk of infection.' One precaution he advocated was the use of easily-destroyed paper handkerchiefs. A year or two earlier the value of Lister's antiseptic treatment in surgery had been recognised by the Amsterdam Congress of 1879, and opened new fields for radical treatment of tuberculosis.

Hassall's bold and original concept had proved a brilliant success. Clayton, writing in 1908, stated that 'upwards of 23,000 sufferers have been benefited with the result that on leaving very many have been able to resume their ordinary occupations. As the hospital is for the admission and relief of patients of all denominations and from every part of the country, it is in the fullest sense a national institution.'[5]

Hassall had taken steps quite early on to ensure that it became a national, not a local, institution by forming a General Committee (of which his brother was a member) with overriding powers in London, in addition to the Local Committee at Ventnor.

In 1877, however, he left Ventnor, remarking that he was very tired by all the journeys to London and by his activities in launching the Hospital. 'I had now resided at Ventnor for a period of nearly ten years during which I had been incessantly occupied, more particularly in the establishment of the hospital, to which object my utmost efforts had been and were still devoted. What with the hospital, my private practice (I had a considerable private practice) . . . laboratory work, my bi-weekly journeys to London, it will not occasion surprise to learn that my health suffered a good deal and that I felt the strain of so much labour both of body and mind, some of which was not unattended with anxiety. On leaving Ventnor, I was presented with a Service of Silver and a purse of three hundred guineas. The Silver bore the following inscription:

This Silver Tray, together with a Tea and Coffee Service, also a purse of
three hundred guineas, were presented
By a numerous body of Subscribers

to

Arthur Hill Hassall M.D.

In recognition of his valuable services as the Originator and Founder of the
Royal National Hospital for Diseases of the Chest
May 1877

After Hassall left, the Hospital continued to grow in size and importance. Comparing the entries in two Directories published sixty years apart, Hill's Directory of 1871[6] states that the hospital occupied a site of over six acres in extent; that had grown to 25 acres in Kelly's Directory of 1935,[7] while the number of patients rose from forty men and women in 1871 to beds for one hundred and sixty-three, eighty-nine for men and seventy-four for women, in 1935. Hospital patients or their relatives were asked to pay 10/− a week, if possible, in 1878, and £2 a week was charged for maintenance in 1935.

Dr Alexander Miller, Physician-Superintendent from 1942 −58, furnished some helpful details about the last years of the Hospital. 'It changed its name by Royal Charter about 1950' he wrote 'dropping Consumption and substituting Diseases of the Chest; it was still treating tuberculosis until its close, although it had begun to take a few convalescent patients from other island hospitals. Surgeons of course had been attached to the Hospital since its foundation,* but in the modern sense surgery began about 1928, Mr Tudor Edwards, one of the pioneers in Thoracic Surgery, being followed by Sir Clement Price Thomas. During the last five years or so surgery was not carried out at the Hospital but concentrated in the Thoracic Surgical Unit at Portsmouth.'

Dr Eric Laidlaw, a consultant at the Isle of Wight Hospital, has been of the greatest help and encouragement during the writing of this book. He informed me that 'he had the doubtful pleasure of presiding over the closing years of the Hospital. It closed on 15 April 1964; the patients remaining were then moved to the Hassall Ward in St Mary's Hospital, Newport,

---

* John B. Martin, M.R.C.S. and H. B. Tuttiet, M.R.C.S. are those named in the original prospectus.

which had been built to replace the original Hospital. A number of the staff also moved to St Mary's – myself included. The Lance Calkin portrait of Hassall is hung at the entrance to the ward. Beneath it is the inscription

Hassall Ward
Opened 12 June 1964
by M. Woodnutt M.P.
This ward is named after Arthur Hill Hassall M.D. the founder in 1868 of the Royal National Hospital Ventnor as a tribute to the work of that Hospital, which now continues here.'

The Lance Calkin portrait was unveiled at the Hospital in 1894, six months after Hassall died, and it is discussed later.

Signor Italo Sabatini of San Remo also painted Hassall's portrait early in 1894. 'This exceedingly fine portrait,' Clayton tells us,[5] 'recently presented to the Hospital by Dr Hassall's widow, (is) now hung in the Board Room at 34 Craven Street, Charing Cross.' It is reproduced as an 'illustration to his *Memoir* (1908) and it is certainly a striking piece of work. Dr Laidlaw observes that the (subsequent) story of the Sabatini portrait 'is sad and baffling. It was brought down to the Hospital after the Charing Cross office was closed in 1948. When the Hospital itself was closed there were a number of portraits of Chairmen, benefactors, etc. hung chiefly in the dining hall; wherever possible the descendants or relatives of the subjects were sought out and the portraits offered to them. So far as I know, the remainder were shown to an art dealer, but few were judged to have sufficient artistic merit to be worth keeping, reconditioning, or offering for sale; the remainder were burnt. It seems likely that the Sabatini Hassall portrait was among those so disposed of.' One of the stained glass windows from the Hospital Chapel which had been installed in the parish church at St Lawrence was dedicated by the Queen Mother on 31 May 1975. Another one was unveiled earlier by Lord Mountbatten when he opened the public gardens on the site of the Hospital.

Hassall it may be certain would be the last person to regret that the Hospital has been closed after almost a century of yeoman service. On the contrary, his keen interest in preventive medicine on which Dr J. N. Blau has commented[8] would be gratified to learn that tuberculosis is now so much under control, a large institute is no longer necessary. Tuberculosis is not the former scourge it was because of the immense improvements in public health and hygiene Hassall was a foremost pioneer to initiate. Moreover, people are better fed, there is an inverse correlation between tuberculosis and nutrition, and here his responsibility for the 1860 Food Adulteration Act continues to play an important part. The site of the Hospital, and the grounds, are now a particularly beautiful public park, haunted by ghosts of the nineteenth-century Europe of kings and emperors. The purpose for which he founded it continues unchanged at the Hassall Ward at St Mary's in the presence of his portrait that once hung in the Hospital dining room.

References for Chapter Ten

1 Geoffrey Boumphorey, Editor, *Shell Guide to Britain*, Ebury Press, 1969.
2 Arthur Mee, *The King's England, Hampshire and the Isle of Wight*, Hodder and Stoughton, 4th Impression 1949.
3 Lawrence Bruce, Reference Librarian, County Library Headquarters, Newport, Isle of Wight.
4 Charles Dickens, *Sketches by Boz: The Hospital Patient.*
5 E. G. Clayton, *A Memoir of the late Dr Arthur Hill Hassall*, Baillière Tindall & Cox, 1908.
6 Hill's *Historical and Commercial Directory of the Isle of Wight*, 1871.
7 Kelly's *Directory of Sandown, Shanklin and Ventnor*, 1935–1936.
8 J. N. Blau *Hassall-Physician and Microscopist, British Medical Journal*, 8 June 1968, 2. 617–619.

ELEVEN
San Remo and Edward Lear

'While at Ventnor,' Hassall tells us, 'I had heard and read of sunny lands in which flowers blossom all the year round, even in the so-called winter months, where orange and lemon trees with their fragrant flowers and golden fruit flourished, and the mountain sides are covered with evergreen olive trees, where date-bearing and other graceful palms abound, and where, in fine, the climate is mild, the scenery enchanting, and where nature appears under its most beautiful aspects and I longed to visit those lands.'

Hassall was tired, his worn crippled body flagging under the load of all that he had packed into the crowded years.

'I determined to give myself a good rest and to pass the remainder of my days in a warmer climate . . . The first year or so were spent chiefly in Germany and one winter season at Cannes. Here I had many influential friends and acquired a certain amount of practice. My success was so encouraging that I thought I would make that flourishing health resort, where my ideal of climate and natural beauty was fully realised, my future home. With that view, I prepared myself for obtaining another medical diploma in order to acquire the right to practise in France. I should have remained there altogether had the examination for the diploma of "Officier de Santé" taken place at the time appointed.

'The postponement of this and the fact that practice in Italy was free to all duly qualified medical men, led me to take up my abode in San Remo, where I have now resided for fifteen winter sessions and which I now regard as my permanent home.

'For the first few years after settling at San Remo, I used to be occupied in London during the summer months, but the necessity to repair there having gradually ceased and as the Swiss medical authorities very liberally and voluntarily conferred upon me the Federal Diploma, I have for the last few

summers practised in Lucerne and still continue to do so, as
also at San Remo in the winter.'

During those first few summers he occupied himself in
London, presumably staying with his brother and his family at
Richmond, he attended meetings of the Hospital General
Committee, shortly to become the Board of Management,
contributed papers to the *Lancet* on the sanitary condition of the
Thames, and continued his interest in matters analytical.
Clayton tells us that he was Public Analyst for the Isle of Wight,
but he must have resigned this appointment on leaving for the
Continent. How far the other laboratories, which changed their
address almost every year, were self-supporting, and how much
he contributed to their upkeep and the salaries of assistants can
only be conjectured. His was the foremost name on the subject,
and they could not have been run at a loss, or he would have
been forced to close them, just as he had to give up a monthly
periodical called *Food Air and Water* which he began to publish at
his own cost about 1874. 'It duly appeared for a long time,' he
tells us, 'but as the expenses were very considerable, the labour
great and the results not encouraging, it was given up.' The
laboratories finally attained a settled address from 1877 on-
wards at 54 Holborn Viaduct, E.C. They were still at the
Viaduct after Hassall died, and here the algal collection found a
home until Clayton handed it over to the British Museum
(Natural History). Further information would be valuable
about Edwy Godwin Clayton, the analytical chemist who met
Hassall rather late in his life, and became so close a friend that
Hassall appointed him sole executor of his Will. I know only
that he was sometime Public Analyst for Fulham and that he
published in 1909 a *Compendium of Food Microscopy*, a work stated
'to have been compiled largely from the works of the late Dr A.
H. Hassall, and constitutes a tribute to the memory of one to
whom food analysts are more deeply indebted than they sometimes realise. The preparation of the book has evidently been a
labour of love, and the author has given a brief summary of the
life-work of Hassall, which will be read with interest by many.'[1]
Clayton's *Memoir of Hassall*[2] is clearly another labour of love,
dedicated to him as a pioneer in Public Hygiene and an untiring
seeker after knowledge, as a token of remembrance and respect.
Unfortunately P. C. Weston, Assistant Editor of *The Analyst*,

has not been able to trace his obituary or even the date on which he died.

In October 1878 Hassall wrote to *The Times* to draw attention to the adulteration of starch, and, a few months later, to the peril of lead in postage stamps. 'If the stamps be moistened with the tongue, hands and lips are quickly stained . . . subjecting a number of penny stamps to analysis I found lead in quantity, doubtless derived from the red lead used in colouring the stamps.' Speedy action by the authorities 'removed all injurious pigments used in colouring stamps.'

Otto Hehner, Hassall's former assistant at Ventnor, reappears to collaborate with him in the Pure Food Company, mentioned in the previous chapter, which did not however prove a success, and the pair burnt their fingers over another project for deplastering wine, removing the burnt gypsum dusted into grape juice from which sherry and some other wines were made, for they infringed a patent taken out by Dr Thudichum and had to pay £50 damages. Hassall, perhaps prompted by memories of his uncle's successful 'Murray's Magnesia', also devised an Invalid Food which met with success until the novelty wore off, when sales dwindled away.

Of greater importance than these projects were the three consecutive summers he spent investigating the value of inhalation in the treatment of respiratory disease, 'aided by the conveniences and appliances of a London laboratory' not named but unlikely to have been one of his analytical establishments. He explored the various methods by which medicaments might reach the lungs; some forms of inhalers he invented 'are,' he says, 'obsolete and useless,' but others yielded striking results, 'first described by me in the *Lancet* for 6 October 1883.' The principles on which an Inhalation Chamber should be constructed were described in an article to the British Medical Association meeting at Liverpool in August 1883, and tested out by building one 'in my house at San Remo. It was completed and in partial operation for a year.' He summed up his results in a book published in 1885 under the title *The Inhalation Treatment of Diseases of the Organs of Respiration.* 'This was, and still is,' (at the time Hassall wrote), 'the only work in the English language devoted exclusively to the subject of the treatment of affections of the lungs by inhalation,

although in America Dr O. Solis Cohen published a separate
book on *Inhalation in the treatment of Disease* as far back as 1867,
while Dr M. J. Oertel brought out a very voluminous work in
1881 entitled *Handbuch der Respiratorischen Therapie* . . . I had
hoped that the publication of my work would have imparted a
new impetus to the practice of inhalation . . . but in these
anticipations I have been disappointed . . . one reason is, that
the busy practitioner cannot afford the time or give the attention necessary to the carrying out of this treatment . . . hitherto
it has not had a full trial on an exact and scientific basis. When
this has been accomplished I am hopeful of beneficial results.'

He suggested trials at a hospital for consumption, but
apparently the hint was ignored at Ventnor, where his successor, Dr Sinclair Coghill, was now firmly established. (In a
speech at the unveiling of the Founder's portrait he remarked
that when he came to the hospital, that now familiar instrument
the thermometer was practically unused and unknown, and
nursing was not what it had now become.)

One treatment for phthisis attracting some attention at that
time, Hassall dismisses briefly. 'Dr Bourgeon's treatment consists,' he says, 'of copious lavements of the sulphuretted mineral
waters of Eaux Bonnes . . . my analyses showed the volume of
dissolved gas to vary within such wide limits although reports
were equally favourable that suspicions arise . . . that any
benefit should be attributed to other causes than the sulphuretted hydrogen . . .'

Other projects that engaged him were a double-necked safety
bottle to avoid swallowing liquids meant for external use only; a
new form of carrying chair; and metal fasteners in lieu of
buttons. He also began to write a special version of the British
Pharmacopoeia which would have paid particular attention to
botany and chemistry, but gave it up when it was anticipated
by Squire's *Companion*. Another work on *Air, Water, and Food* also
never got beyond manuscript stage.

It is clear, reading between the lines of his autobiography,
that he was happiest abroad. Listening may be by the famous
old bridge to the carillons of Lucerne, but above all at San
Remo: 'Being much pleased with San Remo I have now settled
in that place, which has been my home for the last fifteen years,
there I remain and I have no doubt that the climate of the

Western Riviera has been the means of prolonging my life considerably.' He was greatly attracted by the mountains, clothed with blue lavender, girdling Thorenc, twenty miles from Cannes, where he spent the summer and autumn of 1882 in charge of a patient suffering from Bright's disease. But of San Remo he writes, 'I was delighted by my surroundings, the beautiful mountains, the blue Mediterranean, the lovely bays and coves . . . and the semi-tropical vegetation.' Quite soon after his arrival, in 1879 he published a guide *San Remo and the Western Riviera, Climatically and Medically Considered* and followed it up in 1883 by a similar work restricted to San Remo – *Climatically and Medically Considered* – where the climate and topography, natural history, and maladies and diseases for which the climate is suited, are each in turn discussed.

He also embarked upon an exhaustive series of Meteorological observations taken with Negretti and Zambra's thermometers placed in a Stevenson's screen, and carried out for eleven consecutive winter seasons from 1 November to 30 April, covering the years 1879–1890 inclusive. They are recorded in tabular form in his autobiography.

In order to write his first guide, he tells us that he 'began to explore the whole sea-coast, with the many adjacent villages and towns, from Cannes on the one side to Genoa on the other, a distance of about 130 miles . . . Notebook in hand, I jotted down every particular of interest which fell under my observation and each night these rough notes were with my wife's valuable aid put into form with a view to publication when complete.'

Here for the first and last time Hassall mentions a wife in his autobiography, and from evidence presented in the next chapter it is clear he refers to his second wife Alice Margaret. Not Fanny du Corron whom he married in 1846 but the Mrs Hassall named as sole legatee in his Will: 'I give and bequeath to my wife Alice Margaret all and every property and thing of which I may die possessed for her sole use and benefit.'

A century ago there were many colonies of English people dotted round the Riviera and in Italy, living abroad where it was cheaper, while the well-to-do paid annual visits imposed by the social round. Edward Lear, the artist and author of *The Book of Nonsense*, was a neighbour of the Hassall's at San Remo. He had lived there since 1871, moving in 1870 from the Villa Emily to the Villa Tennyson. In September 1885, Lear was on his way home to San Remo when he was taken ill in Lucerne, and Hassall attended him. Sir Franklin Lushington, Barrister, and Fellow of Trinity College, Cambridge, came to stay with him in November, and wrote to Hallam Tennyson from San Remo: 'I won't leave this place without sending you an account of my dear old Lear. He is much better than he was in the summer, and his doctor (Hassall) who at Lucerne thought very ill indeed of his chances of recovery, now says that he may be considered as having "taken out a new lease of life", subject to various conditions which make his life more or less precarious. But he is sadly aged and feeble – totters about within the house – and goes to bed by 6 o'clock . . .'[4]

Hassall's name often appears in those later letters of Lear which Lady Strachey edited[3] (1911). They became friends who had a common interest in the Isle of Wight, for twenty years before Hassall had founded the Ventnor Hospital, Lear had been Queen Victoria's drawing master at Osborne, from 15–18 July inclusive, 1846. At the end of July the Queen returned to London and the lessons were resumed at Buckingham Palace.

Lear wrote to an old friend, Chichester Fortescue, Lord Carlingford, from the Villa Tennyson, San Remo, on 1 December 1885: 'I was afraid you would take cold. *On no account whatever* allow yourself to leave the house without an overcoat. I think I would not pay Doctor Hassall – *till you are sure you are quite well.*'[3]*

Lear wrote to him subsequently, on 6 December 1885: 'Dr Hassall called on me early and told me all about you, and in my opinion you are going on as well as you can expect to be after so violent a chill as you have unluckily taken – along of not dressing according to Italian winter climate which is hot by day and cold at night.'[3] On 19 February 1886 Lear wrote again: 'I was glad to know both from yourself and from Lord Clermont

---

* After a change of Government, Carlingford, who had never recovered from the loss of his wife, resolved to go and see Lear at San Remo; and one afternoon nearing dusk, he sat on a seat out of doors insufficiently clothed for the dangers of the Riviera climate, and dropped off to sleep for a short time. The result was a chill, and the chill was the beginning of a very serious illness and breakdown.[3]

as well as from Mrs Urquhart that you had reached London safely . . . For myself I only grow weaker; but am in no pain, though I have been obliged to send for Hassall this morning owing to return of partial congestion and new threats of bronchitis . . . though the sun is hotter, the wind is colder. Hassall irritates me by his d-d Thermometers and Barometers. As if I couldn't tell when an East wind cuts me in half – spite of the thermometer – by reason of sunshine—being ever so high! I told him just now that I had ordered a baked Barometer for dinner, and 2 Thermometers stewed in treacle for supper.'[3]

And on 11 March 1886: 'I have lost a good deal of acute bronchitis symptoms but am still in bed, congestion of lungs requiring great care day and night. Hassall does all he can.'[3]

At the end of the year Mrs Hassall's name appears.

'December 2 1886 – Mrs Hassall looks in at times, a pleasant and sensible woman. But there is no interchange of thought in these days. Hassall has proved himself an excellent doctor to me.'[3]

During 1887 Sir Franklin Lushington was arranging for the purchase of Lear's painting of Argos by members of Trinity College, Cambridge.[4]

Lear died early the following year, 1888, on the morning of Sunday 29 January.

Among those later letters of Lear's edited by Lady Strachey, she added one from the second Mrs Hassall about Lear's last years. In the preface she remarks '. . . also Madame Philipp, whose first husband was the well-known Dr Hassall of San Remo, both great personal friends of Mr Lear, and the latter also his medical adviser for several years until his death. I have ended this book with a touching letter to myself from Madame Philipp of Lear's last days and death.'[3] The letter, dated 21 January 1911, and headed Nice, runs as follows: 'In the introduction to your delightful book, page xxxii, there is a letter from Mr Lear of 31 July 1870, in which he refers to the form of heart disease from which he suffered for many years and which was primarily the cause of his death. With advancing years he had repeated attacks of bronchitis and bad fits of coughing, with much difficulty of breathing, which greatly distressed him . . . As time went on, poor Mr Lear became weaker and gradually his walks in the garden ceased and at last he re-

mained entirely in his bedroom, finally taking to his bed in
January 1888.

'My first husband, Dr Hassall, was constantly in attendance
on him, and I was continually in and out. Mr Lear did not
complain and was wonderfully good and patient. The day he
died I was there a long time, but he was sinking into uncon-
sciousness and did not know me.

'Dr Hassall and the Rev. H. S. Verschoyle, a great friend of
ours, were with Mr Lear when he died. I was in the room half an
hour before the end, but my husband sent me away, fearing the
last scene might try me too much. It was most peaceful, the
good, great heart simply ceasing to beat. We went of course to
the funeral. I have never forgotten it, it was all so sad, so lonely.
After such a life as Mr Lear's had been and the immense
number of friends he had, there was not one of them able to be
with him at the end.'

Hassall during his last years at San Remo devoted himself to
studies of leaf pigments, chlorophyll in particular, extracting it
in alcohol, and isolating iron from it. Solutions were sent to 'my
friend Edwy Clayton, F.C.S., who also found it contained iron
. . . in autumn when the vitality of the leaves lessens or ceases,
another set of chemical forces comes into operation; the chlorophyll decomposes and the iron is so far liberated as to be free to
enter into other combinations.' The results of his researches
were communicated as a paper on the colours of leaves and
their autumn changes to the Royal Society by the Rt. Hon.
Professor Henry Huxley, read in November 1892. This was not,
of course, his first communication to the Society, for in 1853 and
1854 he had reported on the presence of Indigo in urine and the
reasons for its appearance.

Hassall remained in practice until a few weeks before his
death, which occurred after a short illness on 9 April 1894.

'He was distinguished by a courteous, kindly manner, which
belonged to the old fashioned school, and is regrettably rare at
the present day; "gentleman" was, as someone said of him,
"written largely on his whole bearing." His delicate features
were keenly expressive of the brain, which remained so active to
the last; and his slight, frail figure made the enormous amount
of work which he succeeded in accomplishing, a wonder to men
of sound health.'

So affirms Edwy Clayton, who had evidently found that to know Hassall at all well was to come to love him – and how many others, one wonders had made the same discovery during Hassall's crowded pilgrimage through life, from those far-off days when the 'boy doctor' knelt beside a poor drab in labour on a heap of straw in a fireless room? That incident where he sent his wife away lest the last scene tried her too much is very revealing. Hassall's fame is based most firmly perhaps on those public benefits the result of his tireless investigations with the microscope in more than one field, and with those enquiries in mind, an epitaph for him could not be better framed than on the lines of the following passage, for it expresses so admirably the sentiments that animated him it might have been written with Hassall in mind.

'There can be no more illustrious purpose than that of the research man; to find the truth no matter how obscure; to recognize it no matter in what strange form it may present itself; to formulate it honestly; to state it unmistakably; and to reason from it remorselessly and without regard to prejudice.'[5]

However, Dr J. N. Blau is right to style Hassall Physician and Microscopist,[6] placing Physician first. Hassall tells us that 'success in my profession was my chief aim and desire' and he would be very satisfied to know that Hassall wards in St Mary's, Isle of Wight, and the Royal Free Hospital have been so called to honour his physician's skill.

The Reverend Hamilton S. Verschoyle, the Hassalls' close friend, who had stood with *Doctor* Hassall beside Lear's death-bed, spoke at a Memorial Service held on the first anniversary of Hassall's death, Tuesday, 9 April 1895, at All Saints' Church, San Remo, which was attended by a large number of sympathisers of all nations, many of whom came from a distance, and said, 'I cannot but feel a sad pleasure in being called to speak of one by whose friendship I was honoured. He was one who found delight in constant activity.

'His activity, while that of study did not cease, branched out in three different directions. First, there was the healing of disease. And here, side by side with the intellectual qualities of acuteness in diagnosis, attention to each varying symptom, skill in determining the appropriate remedies, entered the high moral qualities of gentleness and kindness to those in bodily

suffering and weakness; unfailing consideration for and sym-
pathy with those who were suffering the agonies of anxiety. We
felt we had in him, not only the skilled physician, but a true
friend. And the healing of disease he not only sought to carry
out by his own activity as a physician, but through the founding
of the Royal National Hospital for Consumption at Ventnor.

'But not only did he seek to heal disease, he sought to prevent
it, and in this sphere carried out two other great works of his life;
the exposure of adulteration of food and the improvement of the
London water supply, to which may be added his investigations
of the cholera bacillus.

'Yet another great branch of his activity, not only of vast
importance towards prosecution of the other two branches but
as an end in itself, were his scientific studies, pursued in the
interval of his other activities and carried on even in times of
weakness when illness confined him to the house. I remember
well seeing him, at such a time, actively engaged with his
microscope and reagents in the pursuit of his chemical investigations and discoveries on the colours of the leaves of
plants.

'He devoutly worshipped God; he sought in his life to carry
out the will of God; he trusted in Him revealed in Jesus Christ,
and had a "hope full of immortality". Never shall I forget the
devotion, the peace, the bright hopefulness of his last Commun-
ion a few days before his death.

'I do not think that his religion and his science were in two
separate compartments; rather that in his scientific investigations he was realising the words of the Psalmist: "The works of
the Lord are great, sought out of all them that have pleasure
therein", and that on each discovery he made, he would have
joined from his heart in the words of Kepler, when discovering
the laws of the planetary motions, "Oh, my God, I think thy
thoughts after Thee."'

The Memorial Service was conducted by the Rev. H. de
Romestin, Chaplain of All Saints', and at its close 'many of the
congregation proceeded to the cemetery, where the grave of Dr
Hassall presented a striking appearance, the marble slab being
completely hidden by a number of wreaths and crosses of great
beauty.'[2]

I hoped to obtain a photograph of the grave, and accordingly wrote to the present Chaplain, the Rev. Canon D. G. Davies. The following reply was received.

Corso Inglesi 524/3
18038 San Remo (Italy)

December 14, 1974.

Dear Dr Gray:

I am sorry to have taken so long to reply to your letter about Dr Hassall but I can find no record of his burial, nor can I find his grave.

I regret I could not be more helpful.

Yours sincerely,
(signed) David G. Davies.

It is sad that Hassall's marble slab once heaped with floral tributes could not be traced. Lear, who died six years before him, was buried in All Saints' Cemetery too, and Vivien Noakes had his grave photographed (and also that of his manservant) for her *Edward Lear* published 1968.

References for Chapter Eleven

1 *The Analyst*, Review, May 1894.
2 E. G. Clayton, *A Memoir of the late Doctor Arthur Hill Hassall*, Baillière, Tindall & Cox 1908.
3 Lady Strachey, *Later Letters of Edward Lear*, T. Fisher Unwin, London 1911.
4 Vivien Noakes, *Edward Lear*, Collins 1968.
5 *Royal Bank of Canada Monthly Letter*, February 1976 (first published February 1952).
6 J. N. Blau, *Hassall—Physician and Microscopist, British Medical Journal*, 8 June 1968, 2, 617–619.

TWELVE
Who was Mrs Hassall?

Hassall died almost in poverty. His bequest to his widow Alice Margaret was so small she was virtually destitute. Accordingly, perhaps on the advice of Edwy Clayton, her husband's executor – or the suggestion may well have come from Sir Franklin Lushington – she wrote on 14 May 1894, little more than a month after Hassall's death, from their home Corso dell' Imperatrice, San Remo, to the Earl of Rosebery, Premier,* and, about that time, President of the Ventnor Hospital, to ask whether Hassall's Civil List Pension might be extended to her. 'His labours had earned for her husband the title of public benefactor,' she remarked, as was mentioned in Chapter Seven. 'His Pension was conferred on him in recognition of his great public services . . . I now venture to beg . . . that you will have the kindness to advise Her Majesty graciously to continue this pension to myself . . . because of my small and very uncertain means.'[1]

Among those who supported her plea was Sir Richard Quain, who, with Sir George Burrows, had seen Hassall safely through his dangerous illness in 1868, and had since for a time been Consulting Physician to the Hospital, and he did so in the following terms:

'No Civil List pension could possibly have been bestowed on grounds of higher merit than were those that obtained the grant for Dr Hassall. On these grounds his widow has the strongest claim to receive a continuation of the pension; it can scarcely be refused.'[1]

Another powerful champion was Sir Franklin Lushington, who wrote to the Rt. Hon. James Bryce,[1] M.P.:

'Hassall might almost be called the father of modern sanitary science. Bad health obliged him to leave off living in England

* He succeeded Gladstone as Prime Minister in March 1894.

and he settled at San Remo, where he practised up to the time of his death a month ago. He has always enjoyed the highest reputation as a skilful doctor there, but he was not a self-assertive or pushing man, or he probably might have left a larger residue – his own bad health has also stood in the way of a larger practice. He and his wife Mrs Hassall were the kindest of possible friends to my dear old friend Edward Lear during the last years of his life, and that is how I come to know and feel an interest in them.

'Hassall was in middle years when he married, and insured his life for his wife's benefit–a heavy premium, as his health was bad – and after keeping up the policy for 12 or 13 years, the company failed and the whole outlay was lost. The only property left for the widow consists of two villas built by him at San Remo, on one of which a considerable building debt at heavy interest is still outstanding. The only time of year during which a villa can be let at San Remo is from November to May, and it is a very chancy speculation even then.

'The small amount of ready money and fees outstanding at the date of Dr Hassall's death will, I am told, just about to meet the other liabilities exclusive of the building debt. Dr Hassall's name and general merits must be to some extent familiar to Lord Rosebery, as he is now the President of the Hospital at Ventnor of which Dr Hassall was the original founder.'

A copy of Hassall's will had informed me that he left a widow named Alice Margaret, presumably the wife mentioned in his autobiography. But I did not know her maiden name (I still don't know it) and on the meagre data available Somerset House could offer no help, nor the Society of Genealogists, despite the interest taken in the problem by the Secretary. Armed, however, with this information Franklin Lushington supplies in his letter, of a marriage in Hassall's 'middle years' – when he was forty or forty-five, between 1857–62 – Mr Geoffrey Box, who has made similar searches in the past, paid a personal visit to Somerset House on my behalf.

After spending a whole day going through 134 volumes of files, he discovered the entry of the first marriage of Arthur Hill Hassall, Surgeon, at St Pancras in 1846 to Fanny du Corron. No trace, however, was found of a marriage between Hassall and a lady whose Christian names were Alice Margaret. It was

only by going doggedly back through the years from 1870 to
1846 that the existing record was unearthed. Perhaps Hassall
married his second wife abroad – or in Ireland. It would be a
remarkable coincidence – although it is not impossible – if she
was the original Margaret, 'the lady distinguished not only for
an ardent love of nature but as a zealous collector on these
shores whose Christian name I have assigned to this new and
interesting species, Sertularia *Margarete*.'* I have been in touch
with *Oifig an Ard-Chláraitheora*, at *Teach an Chustaim, Baile Átha
Cliath* 1 (Dublin), the Irish equivalent of Somerset House, but
as I did not know the lady's maiden name nor the exact year of
marriage (supposing, of course, one ever was solemnised) I did
not get very far.

At the time Hassall mentions his wife, he was writing the
Riviera Guide published in 1879, when he was sixty-two years
old, and if he married in middle life, he and Alice Margaret had
been together for quite some time. His marriage to Fanny du
Corron, whom he married in 1846 when he was 29, cannot have
lasted more than about a dozen years if he was able to marry
again in his forties.

Alice was granted £50 p.a., half her husband's Civil List
Pension, although the full sum might have been given to his
impoverished widow after all that Hassall had done for the
public. However, in reporting that Lord Rosebery had secured
her that sum, the *Daily Telegraph*, 17 July 1894, and the *Evening
News and Post*, 19 July 1894, briefly refer to her as Mrs Hassall or
'his wife'. No further information about her is forthcoming, and
there is no hint of an earlier marriage.

It was hoped that *The Queen*, 'the lady's newspaper' as it
proudly described itself, might have some personal details
about Alice (or Fanny) to give its feminine audience. But no.
More attention is paid to Hassall's work than one might
imagine its particular readers could digest, yet Alice appears
only as 'she' or Mrs Hassall. Her Christian names, her maiden
name, or her family background, are not given in the relevant
number for 11 August 1894.

At least the Press reports do mention a Mrs Hassall. The
obituaries that appeared earlier that year ignored the surviving

---

* See Chapter Three.

wife with the first one. Admitting that I may not have seen every one, neither Alice Margaret nor Fanny is mentioned in the obituaries in the *Lancet*, 14 April 1894, or the *British Medical Journal* (although both journals state that Richard Hassall was married twice, and to whom, and that he left four children), nor in those obituaries in *The Analyst*, May 1894, the *Westminster Gazette*, 10 April 1894, or the *Guardian*, 18 April 1894. Of course, Richard had married the daughter of an archdeacon, which in those days was socially important, and she was his second wife, so the first one would receive mention as a matter of course. Even so, it is curious that one can read the obituaries of his brother Arthur, whose name was still well-known at the time he died, and who possessed an international reputation (sympathisers of all nations attended the Memorial Service held a year after his death) and never guess that he was married at all, let alone that he married twice.

More strangely still, Alice's name is not recorded amongst those present at the unveiling of the Founder's Portrait by Lance Calkin at the Ventnor Hospital on Monday 15 October 1894, six months after Hassall died. The portrait (the same that hangs today at the entrance to the Hassall Ward at St Mary's Hospital, Newport, I.o.W.) was hung then in the hospital dining room, where it was unveiled. Beneath it was an inscription that may be compared with the present one:

Arthur Hill Hassall
M.D.(London) M.R.C.P.(London)
Founder of this Hospital
Non omnis moriar
Presented by Friends and Subscribers

Mr Neil Horne, the Deputy Chairman, drew attention in his address to the appropriateness of the three words *Non omnis moriar*:* 'I shall not all die. His body lay in the grave at San Remo but his work was there.'[2]

Lance Calkin was among the guests. Born in London on 22 June 1869, he was a portrait painter whose principal works are portraits of H.M. King Edward VII, H.M. King George V,

* *Non omnis moriar, multaque pars mei Vitabit Libitinam* Horatius; Odes III: 30, 6

Marquis Camden and Joseph Chamberlain.[3] It emphasises –
were it necessary – how highly Hassall was esteemed that such
a fashionable artist was commissioned to portray him. Hassall
must have travelled to London for sittings, unless Calkin spent
a winter session at San Remo, in which case he would certainly
have met Mrs Alice Hassall, 'a pleasant sensible woman' as
Edward Lear described her, or if not, he would certainly have
heard about her. What then, one wonders, were his thoughts,
listening to speeches that eulogised Hassall but left the hearers
ignorant that he married twice and that his second wife had
survived him? While to the distant sound of popular airs played
by the band of the Ventnor Volunteers 'in review order on the
south terrace of the gardens' all voices were raised in praise of
Hassall, did no one protest that it was a shame that Mrs Alice
Hassall was not present on that great day?

And when the portrait was at last unveiled, it was not by
Alice, but by the sister of the Chairman of the Board of
Governors, Sir Richard Webster, M.P.[2]

There almost appears to be a conspiracy of silence about
Hassall's wives. Was it embarrassing that although her husband was so famous he left Alice almost penniless? Was the fare
from San Remo to Ventnor not sent to her, lest she turned up for
the ceremony shabbily dressed?

Hassall was portrayed by Signor Sabatini early in 1894 either
because Calkin's portrait was not finished, or he was disappointed by the completed work. Sabatini's portrait is a
vigorous one, judged purely by the reproduction in Clayton's
Memoir. I earlier suggested that it was more lifelike than the one
by Calkin, and Hassall and Alice possibly considered it so.
Clayton is our authority that Alice later presented it to the
Hospital, and it hung for many years in the Board Room at
Charing Cross.

Alice married again some time between 1894, the year of
Hassall's death, and 1911, the year in which she wrote to Lady
Strachey from Nice. It is to be hoped she became Madame
Philipp early rather than late and did not suffer too much
hardship. The name Philipp lacks the final Continental 'e' and
her second husband was possibly English.

Hassall's first wife Fanny, as her maiden name du Corron
suggests, was possibly of French extraction, or her family may

have come from the Channel Islands. She was not, it would appear, married to Hassall for more than a dozen years, and it may be for a much shorter period of time. But she remains even more deeply in the shadows than Alice Margaret, so curiously ignored after Hassall's death.

No family is mentioned in Hassall's Will, but children do not necessarily appear in Wills.

An Albert Hassall M.R.C.V.S. appears in the *Index Catalogue of Medical and Veterinary Zoology* published by the United States of America Department of Agriculture in 1911. He was a Veterinary Inspector of the United States Bureau of Animal Industry, Washington, D.C., but held the English veterinary qualifications M.R.C.V.S. and qualified in 1886 at the London Veterinary College (close by St Pancras Church where Hassall married Fanny du Corron). Born in 1862, no doubt named after the Prince Consort who died the previous December, it is tempting to claim him as a possible son of Arthur Hassall, who would then be forty-five, but it is only a conjecture. Yet it is interesting to find one of that name a member of what the late Professor G. Grey Turner has called the 'sister profession of medicine'.

References for Chapter Twelve

1 Public Records Office, Treasury File T 1/8832 A/9548.
2 E. G. Clayton, *A Memoir of the late Doctor Arthur Hill Hassall*, Baillière, Tindall & Cox 1908.
3 *Who's Who in Art*, Third Edition, The Art Trade Press, London 1934.

Epilogue

An epilogue is defined as 'a speech addressed to the spectators by an actor after a play.' I have been a minor actor in the latest scenes of the story of Arthur Hill Hassall which continues to run – *non omnis moriar* – while the Hassall Wards receive patients, the thymic corpuscles attract notice and the British Museum care for his algal collection.

Many years ago I brought his observations on ciliate protozoa to the attention of the late Professor C. F. A. Pantin, F.R.S., Professor of Zoology at Cambridge University, at that time Reader in Invertebrate Zoology at the University. They were previously unknown to him, but he considered them so remarkable for that early date he sponsored a full time investigation of my own into their activities in Hobsons Brook, a Cambridgeshire chalk stream. As a result, I was able to vindicate all Hassall's conclusions in a paper* which opened with the words 'In 1852 Dr A. H. Hassall etc.' read before the Twelfth International Congress of Limnology in 1953. Hassall little imagined when he examined Thames water under his Ross microscope that his observations would be discussed almost exactly a century later before an audience gathered from all over the world. At Cambridge, too, by a Trinity graduate who had carried out a research programme into his results sponsored by a Fellow of Trinity – the College where John Coppin and Frank Lushington graduated and Frank became a Fellow.

John and Frank were contemporaries, both reading law, so if Hassall did visit John at Trinity, he might well have been introduced to Frank, forty years before they met again at San Remo (and I treasure the thought that Fanny accompanied him).

* E. A. Gray 1955: *The microbiology of a polluted stream*; Proceedings of the International Association of Theoretical and Applied Limnology, vol. XII, 814–817, 1955.

I carried out my programme at the University Botany School under the late Professor of Botany, F. T. Brooks, F.R.S. He was as deeply impressed by Hassall's studies of fungal decay, of which he was unaware until I introduced them to him, as was Dr Pantin by his ciliate studies.

Subsequently I returned to the Botany School to work under the late Professor P. W. Brian, F.R.S., and carry out another microbiological study of the Brook complementary to the first, which would have been incomplete without it, notably as regards ciliate activity. A room was found for me at the Culture Centre of Algae and Protozoa by the kindness of the Director, Mr E. A. George, M.A., an old friend from my first appearance at the Botany School.

I found that my colleagues at the Centre were well acquainted with yet another aspect of Hassall's wide interests, his extensive surveys of British freshwater algae and his book on the subject. Dr D. J. Hibberd, formerly of the Botany Department, British Museum of Natural History, told me much about his algal collection still preserved there.

It was in my student days that the thymic corpuscles first brought Hassall to my notice, although little or nothing was then known as to their function. In my second year, when Student Monitor in Physiology, personal assistant to the Professor, I was awarded a special Certificate of Merit in Histology for some studies of the canine pyramidal tracts which have enabled me to appreciate the practical difficulties Hassall encountered when writing his *Microscopic Anatomy of the Human Body* at a time when the business of fixing and staining tissues was in its infancy.

A doctor of my acquaintance who once asked in his student days who the Hassall was after whom the thymic corpuscles were named, was informed he was 'an eminent physician'. Had my acquaintance referred to the *Narrative of a Busy Life* Hassall has left us, he would have certainly discovered he was an eminent physician, the Hassall Ward at Newport and the Hassall bed at the Royal Free still receive patients, but far more than that; in the last analysis the purity of everything we consume we owe to him. The *Narrative* is exactly what the title promises, the record of the achievements of a most remarkable Victorian pioneer in several fields, the range of whose intellectual curiosity is only matched by that of John Hunter in the previous century, but who has most unjustly been neglected by posterity. It is not, however, an autobiography in the strict sense at all. Only those personal details are given necessary to explain why and where a particular research was carried out, while the story of the early years is slanted to emphasise the difficulties encountered. Hassall had been abroad for fifteen years, out of sight and out of mind at San Remo, when he wrote it to remind a world dazzled by 'the light thrown on the diseases of both the vegetable and animal world' that he had been a solitary pioneer who had anticipated the dawn by the pencil of light streaming through the lenses of his microscope. Edwy Clayton's *Memoir* is penned with the same object in view. The *Narrative* was published only shortly before Hassall's death, and the eighty years that have since elapsed have obscured alike the marble slab in the churchyard of All Saints' Church, San Remo, once heaped with tributary flowers, and the details of his private life. I wrote this sketch of him and his work in the hope of introducing him to a wider public than the present specialised ones, but alas I have gleaned very little about so many of whom only tantalising glimpses are caught in the *Narrative*. Was Fanny waiting for him, perhaps seated in a corner, while the famous photograph was taken of Hassall at his microscope? I would like to know more about Miss Amelia Hunter, and Miss Nolcken, too. And what happened to the young artist Mr Miller – 'that most intelligent young man' – with whom he had walked the crowded evening streets of London, after Hassall finally left London for the Isle of Wight? I shall be richly rewarded if what I have been able to state prompts a biographer better qualified than myself to do the necessary research and Hassall is restored to something approaching the popular esteem he enjoyed when Kingsley mentioned him in *The Water Babies*.

Father of modern sanitary science as Franklin Lushington justly described Hassall, my task has been immensely helped by the details readily forthcoming from those named in the text or chapter references. Doctors, ministers of religion, biologists, librarians, archivists, editors of professional and scientific journals; secretaries of learned societies and University Departments, I appreciate the cordiality met from those approached, and hope apologies may be accepted by any whose names are inadvertently omitted.

I am indebted also to publishers who permitted extracts to be quoted from their publications within the last sixty years and to those who granted permission to quote from official documents, or to reproduce photographs, or who supplied certificates. The letters from which extracts are quoted in Chapter Twelve in respect of Mrs Hassall's pension are contained in a Treasury File T1/8832 A/9548 in the custody of the Public Record Office and are entitled to the same protection as other literary works.

Ernest A. Gray
Cambridge 1982

Appendix A

BIBLIOGRAPHY OF DR. HASSALL'S
PUBLISHED WORKS, PAPERS, Etc

1840–41. A Catalogue of Irish Zoophytes. Published with three plates, in *The Annals and Magazine of Natural History*, vi., 1841, 166, 236.

„ Supplement to Catalogue of Irish Zoophytes, with Description of New Species. Read before the Natural History Society of Dublin, November 6, 1840. Published, with five plates, in *The Annals and Magazine of Natural History*, vii., 1841, 276, 363.

1841. Description of two new Genera of Irish Zoophytes (*Cycloum* and *Sarcochitum*). Communicated to the Dublin Nat. Hist. Soc., February, 1841. *Annals and Magazine of Natural History*, vii., 1841, 483.

1842. On the Phosphorescence of Zoophytes. *Ib.*, viii., 1842, 341.

„ Observations on the Functions performed by the Hairs on the Stigma in *Campanulaceæ, Compositæ*, and other Plants. *Ib.*, viii., 1842, 84.

„ Observations on the Structure of the Pollen Granule, considered principally in Reference to its Eligibility as a means of Classification. *Ib.*, viii., 1842, 92.

„ A list of Invertebrata found in Dublin Bay and its Vicinity. *Ib.*, ix., 1842, 132.

„ Observations on the Structure of the Pollen Granule, considered principally in Reference to its Eligibility as a means of Classification. [Concluded]. With six plates, containing upwards of 150 figures. *Ib.*, ix., 1842, 544.

„ Remarks on the Genus *Lepralia* of Dr Johnston, with Descriptions of Six Undescribed Species, and Notices of Two other Zoophytes (*Discopora verrucaria* and *Madrepora verrucaria*). *Ib.*, ix., 1842, 407.

„ On Showers of Pollen. *Ib.*, ix., 1842, 353.

„ A Critical Examination of Mohl's Views of the

General Structure of the Pollen Granule. *Ib.*, ix., 1842, 93.

1842. A Sketch of the Freshwater Confervæ. Read before the Natural History Society of Dublin. *Ib.*, ix., 1842, 431.

„ Observations on the Genera *Zygnema, Tyndaridea,* and *Mougeotia,* with Descriptions of New Species, *Ib.*, x., 1842, 34.

„ Observations on a New Group (*Vesiculaspermæ*), Genus (*Vesiculifera*), and Sub-Genus (*V. composita*) of Freshwater Confervæ, with Descriptions of Species mostly new. *Ib.*, x., 1842, 336, 385.

„ Observations on the Growth and Reproduction of *Enteromorpha intestinalis.* Read before the Linnæan Society, June 21, 1842. *Proc. Linn. Soc.*, i., 152. *Annals of Natural History,* xi., 1843, 233.

„ An Explanation of the Cause of Rapid Decay of many Fruits, more especially of those of the Apple and Peach Tribes. Read before the Microscopical Society of London, October 19, 1842. *Transactions of the Society,* i., 1844, III. *Annals of Natural History,* x., 1842, 224.

„ On *Plumatella repens. Annals of Natural History,* x., 1842, 153.

„ Further Observations on the Decay of Fruits, more especially of such as belong to the Apple and Peach Tribes. Second paper, read before the Microscopical Society, November 16, 1842. *Transactions of the Microscopical Society,* i., 1844, 116. *Annals of Natural History,* x., 1842, 358.

„ Remarks on a Peculiar Form of Spiral Vessel in the Vegetable Marrow. Paper read before the Microscopical Society, November 16, 1842. *Transactions of the Microscopical Society,* i., 1844, 155; and *Annals of Natural History,* x., 1842, 359.

„ Essay on Distribution, Vitality, Structure, Modes of Growth and Reproduction, and Uses of the Freshwater Confervæ. Read before the Linnæan Society, December 6 and 20, 1842, and February 7, 1843. *Proc. Linn. Soc.*, i, 160, 163. *Annals of Natural History,* xi., 1843, 463.

„ Notice of an Apple in which decay had been artificially induced by inoculation of decayed matter from another apple containing filaments of entophytal fungi. Read before the Linnæan Society, December 20, 1842. *Proc. Linn. Soc.*, i. 160.

1842.   Observations on the Production of Decay in Fruit by Means of Fungi. [Continued.] Read before the Microscopical Society, December 21, 1842. *Transactions of the Society*, i. 119; and *Annals of Natural History*, xi., 1843, 155.

1843.   Some Further Observations on the Decay of Fruit. Fourth Paper on the subject, read before the Microscopical Society, April 19, 1843. *Transactions of the Microscopical Society*, i. 121.

,,   Observations on the Growth, Reproduction, and Species of the Branched Freshwater Confervæ. *Annals of Natural History*, xi., 1843, 359.

Descriptions of British Freshwater Confervæ, mostly New, with Observations on some of the Genera. *Ib.*, xi., 1843, 428.

,,   Remarks on Three Species of Marine Zoophytes. *Ib.*, xi., 1843, 111. [*Antennularia arborescens, Alcyonidium glomeratum*, and *Farcimia spathulosa*.]

,,   Observations on Two of Professor Forbes's 'Retrospective Comments'. *Ib.*, xii., 1843, 117.

,,   Observations on Some Points in the Anatomy and Physiology of the Freshwater Algæ. With a plate. *Ib.*, xii., 1843, 20.

,,   Observations on the Genus *Mougeotia*, on Two New Genera of Freshwater Algæ, and on *Tyndaridea*, with Descriptions of Species. With a plate. *Ib.*, xii., 1843, 180.

,,   Observations on a Disease, the Production of a Fungus, occurring in the Lettuce and other Vegetables. *Ib.*, xii., 1843, 86. Froriep, Notizen, xxviii, 1843, col. 54–56.

1844.   Observations on Ehrenberg's 'De Mycetogenesi Epistola.' *Ib.*, xiii., 1844, 117.

1845.   *A History of the British Freshwater Algæ, including Descriptions of the Desmidiaceæ and Diatomaceæ.* With 103 plates; two vols., 8vo., pp. viii. 486. Samuel Highley.

    Obs.—Later editions of this work appeared, dated

1852 (Taylor, Walton, and Maberley), and 1857 (G. A. Pritzel, *Thes. Lit. Bot.*, 1872: 1852 and 1859, according to B. D. Jackson's *Guide to the Literature of Botany*, 1881).

1845.   On the Failure of the Potato Crop. *Bristol Mercury*, Saturday, October 4, 1845.

„   Uterine Hæmorrhage. *The Lancet*, 1845, i. 186.

„   On a newly discovered Gland in the Human Subject. *Ib.*, 1848, ii. 248.

1848.   Definitions of Three New British Zoophytes. *The Zoologist*, vi., 1848. [*Coppinia, nov. gen.*, sp. *Coppinia mirabilis: Campanularia serpens*; and *Sertularia gracilis*.]

1849.   Observations on the Development of the Fat Vesicle. *The Lancet*, 1849, i. 63.

„   On the Structure of the Papillæ of the Tongue. *Ib.*, 1849, i. 234.

1849.   *The Microscope Anatomy of the Human Body in Health and Disease.* With upwards of 400 illustrations in colour. Two vols., 8vo., pp. xxiv, 570. S. Highley [1846] – 1849.

Obs.—A second edition followed in 1852. American editions appeared in 1851, 1855, and 1869; and in 1852 a German translation by O. Kohlschütter was published at Leipzig. The 'Microscopic Anatomy' contains an account (p. 478) and figures of the cellular bodies in the thymus, known by physiologists as the 'corpuscles of Hassall' (See D. Noël Paton's *Essentials of Human Physiology*, 1907, p. 419, and other standard works, previously cited, p. 4, *ante*).

„   On the Chemistry and Pathology of the Urine. *The Lancet*, 1849, ii. 608, 666, 693.

„   *Observations on the Sanitary Condition of the Norland District, Shepherd's Bush, and Pottery, with suggestions for its Improvement.* Pamphlet, with map. Samuel Highley.

1850.   On the Chemistry and Pathology of the Urine. *The Lancet*, 1850, i. 79, 117, 176.

„   Memoir on the Organic Analysis or Microscopical Analysis of Water supplied to the Inhabitants of London and the Suburban Districts. *Ib.*, 1850, i. 230.

„   *A Microscopic Examination of the Water supplied to the*

Inhabitants of London and the Suburban Districts. Illustrated by twelve coloured plates. S. Highley.

1850. *Evidence, in June,* 1850, *on Water Supply, especially that of the Metropolis.* Report of General Board of Health, 'On the Supply of Water to the Metropolis', 1850, xxii., Appendix No. III. (*Reports and Evidence*), p. 29.

,, On the Colouration of the Water of the Serpentine. Paper read before the Botanical Society of London on July 5, 1850. *The Times,* July 6, 1850; and *The Lancet,* 1850, ii. 64 (quoted from *The Times*).

On the Colouration of Water by Algæ.—Cause of the Colour of the Red Sea. *Lond. Med. Gaz.,* 1850, N.S., xi. 259.

,, *On the Adulteration of Coffee.* Paper read before the Botanical Society of London on Friday, August 2, 1850. *The Times,* Monday, August 5, 1850 (Report).

,, On the Action of the Kidneys. *The Lancet,* 1850, ii. 255.

,, On Certain Points in the Chemistry and Pathology of the Urine. *Ib.,* 1850, ii. 501.

1851. *Evidence before the Select Committee on the Metropolis Water Bills.* Right Hon. Sir James Graham, Bart., in the Chair. July 7, 1851. *Reports from Committees,* 1851, xv. 227.

,, On the Detection of Sugar in the Urine. *The Lancet,* 1851, i. 269.

,, On the Urine, *Ib.,* 1851, i. 403.

,, Report, included in a paper by Dr. Robert Barnes, 'Report on the Anatomy of the Normal Placenta and its Pathological Changes.' *Medico-Chirurgical Transactions,* xxxiv., 1851, 186; and *Medical Times,* New Series, Vol. ii., 1851, 218.

,, Descriptions of Three Species of Marine Zoophytes by A. H. Hassall, F.L.S., and John Coppin, M.A. Paper read before the Microscopical Society, April 16, 1851. *Transactions* of the Society, iii., 1852, 160. (*Coppinia mirabilis, Campanularia serpens, and Sertularia gracilis.*)

,, The University of London Committee of Graduates. *The Lancet,* 1851, i. 534.

1851-52-53-54. *Series of Reports on the Adulteration of Food, Drink and Drugs.* (Published under the title of the 'Analytical

Sanitary Commission.') *The Lancet*, 1851-52-53-54.

1851.   On the General Occurrence of the Sugar Acarus. [In
Report on Sugar.] *Ib.*, 1851, i. 77.

,,   On the Character and Growth of the Yeast Plant. [In
Report on Bread.] *Ib.*, 1851, i. 391.

"   Description of the remarkable bodies in the Cocoa-
Seed, now known to be multicellular hairs, and sometimes named 'Mitscherlichian bodies', after the supposed first discoverer. [In Report on Cocoa.] *Ib.* 1851, i.
553-554.

Obs.—Dr Hassall observed and described these
bodies many years before Mitscherlich; in justice
they should in future be termed '*Hassallian* bodies'.

1852.   On the Detection and Preservation of Crystalline
Deposits of Uric Acid, Urate of Ammonia, Phosphate
of Lime, Triple Phosphate, Oxalate of Lime, and other
Salts. *Ib.*, 1852, i. 466, 567.

"   Microscopical Investigations for Dr W. Tyler
Smith's 'Memoir on the Pathology and Treatment of
Leucorrhœa, based on the Microscopic Anatomy of the
Os and Cervix Uteri.' *Medico-Chirurgical Transactions*,
xxxv., 1852, 377.

"   On the Development of Torulæ in the Urine, and on
the Relation of these Fungi to Albuminous and Sac-
charine Urine Paper read before the Royal Medical and
Chirurgical Society, Tuesday, November 23, 1852.
Medico-Chirurgical Transactions, xxxvi., 1853, 23: and *The
Lancet*, 1852, ii. 531.

"   Letter on the same subject. *The Lancet*, 1852, ii. 581.

1853.   On Certain Important Points in the Chemistry of the
Urine. *Ib.*, 1853, i. 9, 338, 362.

Review of Dr Golding Bird's work on Urinary Deposits. *British and Foreign Medico-Chirurgical Review*, xii.,
1853, 123.

"   On a remarkable Case of *Sarcina Ventriculi*. Paper read
before the Medical Society of London, January 22,
1853. *The Lancet*, 1853, i. 119; and *Medical Times*, New
Series, vi., 1853, 127.

"   *On the Occurrence of Indigo in the Urine.* Paper read
before the Royal Society, June 16, 1853. *Abst. Phil.
Trans.*, 1850–54, vi. 327; and *The Lancet*, 1853, ii. 320.

1853.   Cases under the care of Dr Hassall (at the Royal Free Hospital). *The Lancet*, 1853, ii. 385.

1854.   On the Development of Vibriones in Urine. Paper read before the Royal Medical and Chirurgical Society, Tuesday, June 27, 1854. *The Lancet*, 1854, ii. 10.

„   *On the Frequent Occurrence of Indigo in Human Urine, and on its Chemical, Physiological, and Pathological Relations.* Paper read before the Royal Society, June 15, 1854. *Phil. Trans.*, vol. cxliv., parts 1, 2, p. 297; *Journ. de Pharm.*, xxv., 1854, 357; and *The Lancet*, 1854, ii. 443.

„   *Evidence before Parliamentary Select Committee on Public-houses,* June 23, 1854. Right Hon. C. P. Villiers, M.P., Chairman. May–July, 1854. *Reports from Committees,* 1854, xiv.

„   *Reports, dated December* 21, 1854, *containing the Results of the Microscopical Examination of Different Waters, principally those used in the Metropolis . . . during the Cholera Epidemic in* 1854. Illustrated with twenty-five coloured plates. Appendix to Report of Committee for Scientific Inquiries in Relation to the Cholera Epidemic in 1854. *General Board of Health,* Reports of Commissioners, 1854–55, xxi.

1854–55.   *Reports containing the Results of the Microscopical Examination of the Rice-water Evacuations* (December, 1854), *the Urine, the Blood, and the Skin of Cholera Patients* (January, 1855); *also of the Air Respired and the Clothes Worn* (January 22, 1855). Illustrated with Figures. Appendix to Report of Committee for Scientific Inquiries in Relation to the Cholera Epidemic of 1854. *General Board of Health.* Reports of Commissioners, 1854–55, xxi.

Obs.—In a 'Letter of the President of the General Board of Health (Sir Benjamin Hall, Bart., M.P.) to the Right Hon. the Viscount Palmerston, Secretary of State for the Home Department,' dated 1855, 'accompanying a Report from Dr Sutherland on Epidemic Cholera in the Metropolis in 1854,' there are numerous references to Dr Hassall's investigations, with extracts from his opinions and recommendations.

1855.   *Food and Its Adulterations*, one vol., 8vo., pp. xlviii, 659, and 159 engravings. Longmans and Co.

    Obs.—In 1856 a German treatise on the same subject, 'Die Verfälschung der Nahrungsmittel und Getränke', based largely on Dr Hassall's book, was produced by P. F. H. Klencke, and published at Leipzig.

     "   On Food and Its Adulteration. *The Times*, July 27, 1855.

     "   On Food and Its Adulteration, *Ib.*, July 31, 1855.

     "   How Bottled Fruits and Vegetables are made Green. *Ib.*, August 1, 1855.

     "   On the Chemistry of the Adulteration of Food. Paper read before the British Association at Glasgow (Chemical Section), on Monday, September 17, 1855. *The North British Daily Mail*, September 18, 1855.

     "   On the Adulteration of Annatto. Paper read before the Pharmaceutical Society, Wednesday, December 5, 1855. *Pharmaceutical Journal*, xv., 1856, 295.

1855–56.   *Evidence before Parliamentary Select Committee appointed to Inquire into the Adulteration of Food, Drinks, and Drugs.* William Scholefield, Esq., M.P., Chairman. Dr Hassall's evidence was given on July 13 and 18, 1855, and May 2, 1856. *Reports from Committees*, 1854–55, viii., and 1856, viii.

1856.   On the Adulteration of Liquorice, Paper read before the Medical Society of London, April 11, 1856. *The Lancet*, 1856, i. 458.

     "   On the Adulteration of Food. *The Times*, April 19, 1856.

     "   Liebig on Alum in Bread. *The Times*, August 23, 1856.

1857.   On Allen *v.* The Chester and Holyhead Railway. *The Times*, February 20, 1857.

     "   On the great Tobacco Question. *The Lancet*, 1857, i. 197.

     "   Case under the care of Dr Hassall. *Ib.*, 1857, i. 424.

     "   Report on the Bread of Edinburgh. *The North Briton*, May 30, and June 6, 13, and 20, 1857.

     "   Report on the Oatmeal of Edinburgh. *The North Briton*, July 15 and 23, 1857.

     "   *Report*, dated January 31, 1857, *on the Microscopical*

Examination of the Metropolitan Water Supply. Addressed to the Right. Hon. William Cowper, M.P., President of the General Board of Health.—*Accounts and Papers*, 1857, xiii. 149; and *The Lancet*, 1857, i. 467.

1857. *Report, Microscopical and Chemical, on the Water of the Serpentine.* May, 1857. Drawn up at the request of Sir Benjamin Hall, Bart., M.P.—General Board of Health, 1857. Parliamentary Papers, 1857, xli. 241; and (Extract) *The Lancet*, 1857, ii. 60.

" *Adulterations Detected in Food and Medicine.* Longmans and Co., 1857; pp. xvi.712; and 225 engravings.

" The Glasgow Case. The Microscope. *The Lancet*, 1857, ii. 71. [Note on Madeleine Smith Case.]

" On Arsenite of Copper. *The Lancet*, 1857, ii. 407.

1858. Microscopical Report on the Thames Water at Richmond. Embodied in 'A Letter to the Churchwardens of Richmond, Surrey, having Reference . . . more especially to the Water-Supply,' by Richard Hassall, M.D., January, 1858.

" A Practical Course of Lectures on Urinary Disorders. *The Lancet*, 1858, i. 1, 53, 105, 157, 233, 283, 333, 381, 429, 499, 523, 549, 573, 623.

" On Stone in the Bladder. *Ib.*, 1858, ii. 197.

" On Adulterations. *The Times*, November 11, 1858. [Relating chiefly to adulterations of lozenges and confectionery.]

1859. *The Urine in Health and Disease.* With 24 plates, 12°., pp. viii, 82, Churchill and Sons, 1859.

" How Adulteration is Punished in France. *The Times*, February 1, 1859.

" On Arsenical Paper-Hangings. *The Lancet*, 1859, i. 70.

" Diabetes Successfully Treated. *Ib.*, 1859, i. 385.

" Arsenical Pigments in Paper-Hangings. Ib., 1859, ii. 95.

" On the Development and Signification of *Vibrio lineola, Bodo urinarius* . . . in Alkaline and Albuminous Urine. *Ib.*, 1859, ii. 503–6.

Obs.—The species of *Bodo* (*B.urinarius*) discovered by Dr Hassall, and described in this paper, is referred to in R. Leuckart's *Die Menschlichen Parasiten*, 263, vol.

i., p. 144; see also *Schmidt's Jahrbücher*, cix. 1861, p. 157; and W. E. Hoyle's translation (1886) of Leuckart's work.

1859.   Case under the care of Dr Hassall. *Ib.*, 1859, ii. 535.

1859–60. *On the Frequent Occurrence of Phosphate of Lime, in the Crystalline Form, in Human Urine, and on its Pathological Importance.*—Communicated to the Royal Society by Dr Sharpey. Received November 7, 1859, and read January 26, 1860. *Proc. Royal Soc.* x. 281.

1860.   *Evidence before the Parliamentary Select Committee on the Serpentine*, March 22, 1860. Chairman, Right Hon. Wm. Fras. Cowper, M.P.—Parliamentary Papers, 1860, xx. 1, and Appendix 7; also *The Lancet*, 1860, i. 212, 268.

,,   Article, 'Adulteration, and its Remedy'. *Cornhill Magazine*, July, 1860.

,,   On the Injurious Effects of White Lead as a Paint. *The Lancet*, 1860, i. 229.

,,   On Unexpected Sources of Lead Poisoning. *Ib.* 1860, i. 357.

,,   On the Danger of Green Paint in Artificial Leaves and Flowers. *Ib.*, 1860, ii. 535.

,,   Letters on the subject of Adulteration. Messrs. J. Travers and Sons' *Circular*, April 5, 16, 24, and 30, and May 8, 1860. [Quoted in *The Times* of September 11, 1860.]

1861.   Pure Mustard. *The Lancet*, 1861, ii. 621. [Letter advocating the sale of mustard unmixed with farinaceous matter.]

,,   *Adulterations detected in Food and Medicine*, 2nd edition. Longmans and Co., pp. xvi, 712, and 225 engravings.

1862.   Report *On Paraffin Oil: Its Impurities and Adulterations* (*The Lancet* Analytical Sanitary Commission). *The Lancet*, 1862, i. 333.

,,   Milk. *The Times*, December 29, 1862.

1863.   Observations on the Employment in the Arts of Scheele's Green, or Arsenite of Copper, and other Metallic Pigments. *The Lancet*, 1863, i. 204.

,,   *The Urine in Health and Disease*, pp. xiii, 416, and 79 engravings, many coloured by hand. 8vo. Second edition. Churchill and Sons, 1863.

1864.   Paraffin and Petroleum Oils. *The Standard*, February 17, 1864.

,,   Paraffin and Petroleum Oils. *Ib.*, February 20, 1864.

,,   On the Sugar Duties. *The Times*, April 21, 1864.

,,   The Medical Officer of Health for St Marylebone. *The Lancet*, 1864, ii. 307.

,,   On Pyelitis, or Abscess of the Kidney. *Ib.*, 1864, ii. 544.

,,   Clinical Remarks on Cases of Bright's Disease. *Ib.*, 1864, ii. 681.

,,   On the Action of Tincture of Perchloride of Iron in the Cure of Renal and Urinary Affections. *Ib.*, 1864, ii. 740.

1865.   On the Determination of Chlorine and Urea in the Urine by Liebig's Method with Protonitrate of Mercury, Part I. *Ib.*, 1865, i. 170.

,,   The same, continued. *Ib.*, 1865, i. 196.

,,   On the Estimation of Uric Acid, and on the Amount contained in Human Urine. *Ib.*, 1865, i. 471.

,,   The same, continued. *Ib.*, 500.

,,   The same, continued. *Ib.*, 528.

,,   The same, concluded, *Ib.*, 646.

,,   Abstract of the same Communication. *Chemical News*, xii., 1865, 25–26.

,,   *On the Nutritive Value of Liebig's Extract of Beef, Beef-Tea, and of Wine. Ib.*, 1865, ii. 49. [Letter expressing doubt as to the alleged nutritive value of Liebig's Extractum Carnis.]

,,   Liebig's Food for Infants and Invalids. *Ib.*, 1865, ii. 135.

,,   On Intermittent or Winter Hæmaturia. *Ib.*, 1865, ii. 368.

,,   Liebig's Extract of Meat. *Ib.*, 1865, ii. 486.

,,   On the Curability of Bright's Disease. *Ib.*, 1865, ii. 670.

1866.   On the Concentration and Preservation of Meat. *Ib.*, 1866, i. 185. [Describing a preparation, *Flour of Meat*.]

,,   On Flour of Meat. *Ib.*, 1866, i. 469. [Further communication on the same subject.]

,,   Brian Biscuits in Diabetes. *Ib.*, 1866, i. 640.

,,   The same. *Ib.*, 1866, i. 719.

1867.   On the Quality of the Water supplied to the Town of

APPENDIX A 167

Ventnor. Letter, dated June 4, 1867. *Isle of Wight Advertiser*, Saturday, June 8, 1867.

1867. Representation of the London University. *The Lancet*, 1867, ii. 56. [Letter deprecating political considerations in the choice of a parliamentary representative of the University.]

1868. On the Punishment for Adulteration in the Middle Ages: Pillory, Hurdle, etc. *Ib.*, 1868, ii. 154.

,, Flour of Meat. *Ib.*, 1868, ii. 716.

1870. *Appeal for the Ventnor Hospital for Consumption. The Times*, January 24, 1870.

1871. State of the Metropolitan Waters. *Ib.*, 1871, i. 322.

,, Various 'Analytical Records,' contributed to *The Lancet*, and extending over a series of years; 1871, *et cetera*.

1872. The Ventnor Consumption Hospital. *The Lancet*, 1872, i. 238.

,, Health Officers as Public Analysts. *Ib.*, 1872, ii. 689.

,, Officers of Health as Food Analysts. *Ib.*, 1872, ii. 761.

,, Liebig's Extract of Meat. *Food, Water, and Air*, ii., 1872, 3.

1873. The Emperor Napoleon. *Ib.*, 1873, i. 113.

,, On Adulteration. *The Times*, June 24, 1873.

,, The Inland Revenue Board and the Adulteration of Chicory. *The Lancet*, 1873, i. 220.

,, On Adulterated Mustard. *The Times*, October 15, 1873.

1871–74. *Food, Water, and Air*. [A Sanitary Journal, founded and edited by Dr Hassall.]

1874. *Evidence before Parliamentary Select Committee on the Adulteration of Food Act*, 1872, on Thursday, June 18, 1874. Chairman, Clare Sewell Read, Esq., M.P. *Reports from Committees*, 1874, vi., p. 305.

,, On the Adulteration of Tea. *The Times*, January 9, 1874.

,, On the Manufacture of Sherry. *Ib.*, March 4, 1874.

,, On the Adulteration of Food. *Ib.*, May 26, 1874.

,, The same. *Ib.*, June 8, 1874.

1875. Letters on Professional Etiquette. *The Lancet*, 1875, i. 426, 494, 596.

,, On the Alimentation of Infants, Children, and Invalids. Pamphlet: Goodall, Backhouse and Co., Leeds.

1875.   On (faced) Green Tea. *The Times*, October 27, 1875.
  ,,   On the Adulteration Acts. *Ib.*, November 13, 1875.
1876.   *Food. Its Adulterations and the Methods for their Detection.*
One vol., 8vo., pp. viii, 896, and 206 engravings.
Longmans and Co., 1876.
1878.   Five Reports on the Food Exhibits at the Paris
Exhibition. *The Lancet*, 1878, ii. 306, 344, 416, 453, 491.
  ,,   Report on the Wells of Henley-upon-Thames. *Ib.*,
413.
  ,,   Reports on the Sanitary State of the Thames, and
Condition of the River. *Ib.*, 526, 562, 601.
  ,,   Notes on San Remo. *The Lancet*, 1878, ii. 616.
  ,,   The Adulteration of Starch. *The Times*, October 5,
1878.
1879.   The Ventnor Hospital. *The Lancet*, 1879, i. 426.
  ,,   On Postage Stamps. *The Times*, June 2, 1879.
  ,,   On the Decline of Adulteration. *The Times*, September 3, 1879.
  ,,   On Davos Platz. *The Lancet*, 1879, ii. 152.
  ,,   *San Remo and the Western Riviera.* One vol., 8vo., pp.
xiv, 279, with frontispiece, map, and engravings. Longmans and Co.
1880.   The Sunny South. *The Lancet*, 1880, i. 70.
  ,,   On Lead in Stamps. *The Times*, July 20, 1880.
  ,,   On the Winter Climate of San Remo. Paper presented to the Section of Medicine, British Medical
Association, Annual Meeting at Cambridge, August
1880. *British Medical Journal*, 1880, ii. 542.
1881.   On Frothing Urine. *British Medical Journal*, 1881, i.
767.
  ,,   The Climate of the Riviera. Paper, International
Medical Congress, Seventh Session, London, 1881, ii.
185–189.
  ,,   The Winter Climate of San Remo. *Ib.*, 1881, ii. 659.
  ,,   On a Form of Dyspepsia Occurring in Infants, *The
Lancet*, 1881, ii. 941.
1882.   On the Necessity for the Disinfection of Clinical
Thermometers. *Ib.*, 1882, i. 83.
  ,,   On the Winter Climate of San Remo. *British Medical
Journal*, 1882, ii. 622.
1883.   *San Remo Climatically and Medically Considered.* One

vol., 8vo., xi, 290 pp., with illustrations. Longmans and Co.

1883.   On Inhalation, more particularly Antiseptic Inhalation, in Diseases of the Lungs. A paper read before the Fifty-first Annual Meeting of the British Medical Association at Liverpool, Friday, August 3, 1883. *British Medical Journal*, 1883, ii. 869.

"   On the Comparative Inutility of Antiseptic Inhalation, as at present practised in Phthisis and other Diseases of the Lungs. *The Lancet*, 1883, i. 765, 1067.

"   On Inhalation. *Ib.*, 1883, ii. 580.

1884.   Construction of Chambers for Inhalation. *Ib.*, 1884, i. 106; and *British Medical Journal*, 1884, i. 46.

"   Inhalation in Pulmonary Affections. *British Medical Journal*, 1884, i. 89.

"   On Investigations into the Nature of Cholera. *The Lancet*, 1884, ii. 38, 167, 847.

"   A New Form of Inhaler. *The Lancet*, 1884, ii. 273.

1885.   *The Inhalation Treatment in Diseases of the Organs of Respiration, including Consumption.* One vol., 8vo., pp. viii, 367, with engravings. Longmans and Co.

"   On the Health of San Remo. *The Lancet*, 1885, ii. 837; and *British Medical Journal*, 1885, ii. 842.

1886.   On a New Method of Inhalation and a New Form of Apparatus. *The Lancet*, 1886, i. 192.

"   The Disinfection of the Sputum of Phthisis. *British Medical Journal*, 1886, i. 566.

1887.   On Bergeon's New Method of Treating Consumption. *The Lancet*, 1887, ii. 10.

1888.   Ventnor Hospital. *The Lancet*, 1888, i. 456.

"   Hypodermic Syringes. *British Medical Journal*, 1888, ii. 522.

1889.   On Sputa. *The Lancet*, 1889, ii. 162.

1890.   English and Foreign Health Resorts. *British Medical Journal*, 1890, i. 153.

"   On the Alleged Increase of Consumption at San Remo. *Ib.*, 1104, 1332.

"   On Safety Bottles. *Ib.*, 1375.

"   A New Form of Carrying-Chair. *Ib.*, ii. 850.

"   *On the Climate of San Remo*, based on the Observations of Ten Consecutive Winter Seasons. Paper presented on Tuesday, August 1, to the Fifty-eighth Annual Meeting of the British Medical Association at Birmingham, July and August 1890. *Ib.*, 1890, ii. 342. [See *infra*, Appendix to '*The Narrative of a Busy Life*.']

1891. On the Use of Pocket Handkerchiefs by the Phthisical. *Ib.*, 1891, i. 1055.

1892. *On the Colour of Leaves of Plants and their Autumnal Changes.* Paper communicated to the Royal Society by the Right Hon. Professor Huxley, F.R.S., received June 21, and read November, 1892. *Proc. Royal Soc.*, lii. (1893), 276; and *Appendix* to '*The Narrative of a Busy Life*,' 1893.

,, *On the Colouration of the Leaves of Plants.* Further paper communicated to the Royal Society, received November 15, 1892. Appendix to '*The Narrative of a Busy Life*,' 1893.

,, San Remo as a Winter Resort. *British Medical Journal*, 1892, i. 290.

1893. *The Narrative of a Busy Life.* An Autobiography. [With an Appendix, including the above-mentioned papers, '*On the Climate of San Remo*', '*On the Colour of the Leaves of Plants and their Autumnal Changes*', and '*On the Colouration of the Leaves and Plants*.'] One vol., 8vo., pp. iii, 166, 82. Longmans and Co., 1893.

Appendix B

Regulations for the M.B. and M.D. degrees of the University of
London, from the University Calendar of 1851
(by courtesy of the Librarian, University of London Library)

BACHELOR OF MEDICINE

Candidates for the Degree of Bachelor of Medicine shall be
required

1. To have been engaged during Four Years in the professional studies
at one or more of the Institutions or Schools recognised by this University.

2. To have spent One Year at least, of the Four, in one or more of the
recognised Institutions or Schools in the United Kingdom.

3. To pass Two Examinations.

FIRST EXAMINATION

The FIRST EXAMINATION shall take place once a year, and
commence on the first Monday in August*.

No Candidate shall be admitted to this Examination unless
he have produced Certificates to the following effect:

1. Of having completed his Nineteenth year.

2. Of having taken a Degree in Arts in this University, or in a University
the Degrees granted by which are recognised by the Senate of this
University†; or of having passed the Matriculation Examination‡.

3. Of having been a Student during Two Years at one or more of the
Medical Institutions or Schools recognised by this University, subsequently to having taken a Degree in Arts, or passed the Matriculation Examination.

4. Of having attended a Course of Lectures on each of Four of the
subjects in the following list:

---

* The annual number of Examinations will be increased at a future period, should it
be found desirable.

† The Degrees in Arts of all Universities in the United Kingdom are recognised by
the Senate for this purpose.

‡ The Matriculation Examination is the same for Students in Arts and for Students
in Medicine.

DESCRIPTIVE AND SURGICAL ANATOMY.
GENERAL ANATOMY AND PHYSIOLOGY.
COMPARATIVE ANATOMY.
PATHOLOGICAL ANATOMY
CHEMISTRY.
BOTANY.
MATERIA MEDICA AND PHARMACY.
GENERAL PATHOLOGY.
GENERAL THERAPEUTICS.
FORENSIC MEDICINE.
HYGIENE.
MIDWIFERY AND DISEASES PECULIAR TO WOMEN AND INFANTS.
SURGERY.
MEDICINE.

5. Of having Dissected Nine Months.

6. Of having attended a Course of Practical Chemistry, comprehending Practical Exercises in conducting the more important processes of General and Pharmaceutical Chemistry; in applying Tests for discovering the Adulteration of articles of the Materia Medica, and the presence and nature of Poisons; and in the examination of Mineral Waters, Animal Secretions, Urinary Deposits, Calculi, &c.

7. Of having attended to Practical Pharmacy during a sufficient length of time to enable him to acquire a practical knowledge in the Preparation of Medicines.

These Certificates shall be transmitted to the Registrar at least fourteen days before the Examination begins.

The Fee for this Examination shall be Five Pounds. No Candidate shall be admitted to the Examination unless he have previously paid this Fee to the Registrar. If a Candidate fail to pass the Examination, the Fee shall not be returned to him; but he shall be afterwards admissible to the First Examination without the payment of any additional Fee.

Candidates shall be examined in the following subjects:

ANATOMY.
PHYSIOLOGY.
CHEMISTRY.
BOTANY.*
MATERIA MEDICA AND PHARMACY.

---

* For a syllabus of this subject, see pages 70 and 71.

The Examinations shall be conducted in the following order:

Morning, 10 *to* 1.

Monday . . . Anatomy and Physiology, by Printed Papers.
Tuesday . . . Chemistry, by Printed Papers.
Wednesday, 10 *to* 12 . . . Botany, by Printed Papers.

Afternoon, 3 *to* 6.

Monday . . . Anatomy and Physiology, by Printed Papers.
Tuesday . . . Materia Medica and Pharmacy, by Printed Papers.

To commence on Friday, at 10.

Chemistry, by *Vivâ Voce* and Experiment: and Materia Medica and Pharmacy, by *Vivâ Voce* and Demonstration from Specimens.

To commence on Tuesday, in the following week, at 10.

Anatomy and Physiology, by *Vivâ Voce*, Demonstration from Preparations, and Dissection.

On Wednesday Morning in the week following the commencement of the Examination, the Examiners shall arrange in Two Divisions, each in alphabetical order, such of the Candidates as have passed; and a Pass Certificate, signed by the Registrar, shall be delivered to each Candidate.

Such Candidates only as in the opinion of the Examiners are admissible to the Examination for Honours, shall be placed in the First Division.

EXAMINATION FOR HONOURS.

Any Candidate who has been placed in the First Division at the First Examination may be examined for Honours in any or all of the following subjects:

ANATOMY AND PHYSIOLOGY.
    Candidates may illustrate their answers by sketching the parts they describe.
CHEMISTRY.
MATERIA MEDICA AND PHARMACEUTICAL CHEMISTRY.
STRUCTURAL AND PHYSIOLOGICAL BOTANY.*

* See the "*N.B.*" in page 71.

The Examinations shall take place in the week following the commencement of the First Examination. They shall be conducted by means of Printed Papers; but the Examiners shall not be precluded from putting *vivâ voce* questions upon the written answers of the Candidates when they appear to require explanation.

The Examinations shall be conducted in the following order:

Morning, 10 to 1.

Thursday . . . Anatomy and Physiology.
Friday . . . Chemistry.
Saturday . . . Structural and Physiological Botany.

Afternoon, 3 to 6.

Thursday . . . Anatomy and Physiology.
Friday . . . Materia Medica and Pharmaceutical Chemistry.

In determining the relative position of Candidates, the Examiners shall have regard to the proficiency evinced by the Candidates in the same subjects at the Pass Examination.

Candidates who pass the Examinations, and acquit themselves to the satisfaction of the Examiners, shall be arranged according to the several subjects and according to their proficiency in each; and Candidates shall be bracketed together, unless the Examiners are of opinion that there is a clear difference between them.

If in the opinion of the Examiners sufficient merit be evinced, the Candidate who shall distinguish himself the most in Anatomy and Physiology, the Candidate who shall distinguish himself the most in Chemistry, and the Candidate who shall distinguish himself the most in Materia Medica and Pharmaceutical Chemistry, shall each receive an Exhibition of Thirty Pounds per annum for the next Two Years.

Under the same circumstances, the First and Second Candidates in each of the preceding subjects shall each receive a Gold Medal of the value of Five Pounds.

Under the same circumstances, the Candidate who shall distinguish himself the most in Structural and Physiological Botany shall receive a Gold Medal of the value of Five Pounds.

SECOND EXAMINATION

The SECOND EXAMINATION shall take place once a year, and commence on the first Monday in November.

No Candidate shall be admitted to this Examination within Two academical Years of the time of his passing the First Examination, nor unless he have produced Certificates to the following effect:

1. Of having passed the FIRST EXAMINATION.

2. Of having, subsequently to having passed the FIRST EXAMINATION, attended a Course of Lectures on each of Two of the subjects comprehended in the list at page 59, and for which the Candidate had not presented Certificates at the FIRST EXAMINATION.

3. Of having, subsequently to having passed the FIRST EXAMINATION, Dissected during Six Months.

4. Of having conducted at least Six Labours.
   Certificates on this subject will be received from any legally-qualified Practitioner in Medicine.

5. Of having attended the Surgical Practice of a recognised Hospital or Hospitals during Twelve Months, and Lectures on Clinical Surgery.

6. Of having attended the Medical Practice of a recognised Hospital or Hospitals during other Twelve Months, and Lectures on Clinical Medicine.

7. Of having, subsequently to the completion of his attendance on Surgical and Medical Hospital Practice, attended to Practical Medicine in a recognised Hospital, Infirmary, of Dispensary, during Six Months.
   Certificates on this subject will be received from any legally-qualified Practitioner having the care of the poor of a parish.

The Candidate shall also produce a Certificate of Moral Character from a Teacher in the last School or Institution at which he has studied, as far as the Teacher's opportunity of knowledge has extended.

These Certificates shall be transmitted to the Registrar at least fourteen days before the Examination begins.

The Fee for this Examination shall be Five Pounds. No Candidate shall be admitted to the Examination unless he have previously paid this Fee to the Registrar. If a Candidate fail to pass the Examination, the Fee shall not be returned to him; but he shall be afterwards admissible to the Second Examination without the payment of any additional Fee.

Candidates shall be examined in the following subjects:

PHYSIOLOGY.
The papers in Physiology shall include questions in Comparative Anatomy.
GENERAL PATHOLOGY, GENERAL THERAPEUTICS, HYGIENE.
SURGERY.
MEDICINE.
MIDWIFERY.
FORENSIC MEDICINE.

The Examinations shall be conducted in the following order:

FIRST WEEK. *By Printed Papers.*

Morning, 10 *to* 1.

Monday . . . Physiology.
Tuesday . . . Surgery.
Wednesday . Midwifery.

Afternoon, 3 *to* 6.

Monday . . . General Pathology, General Therapeutics, Hygiene.
Tuesday . . . Medicine.
Wednesday . Forensic Medicine.

SECOND WEEK. *By Vivâ Voce Interrogation.*

To commence on Monday Morning, at 10.

On Monday Morning in the following week the Examiners shall arrange in Two Divisions, each in alphabetical order, such of the Candidates as have passed. And a Certificate under the Seal of the University, and signed by the Chancellor, shall be delivered to each Candidate.

Such Candidates only as in the opinion of the Examiners are admissible to the Examination for Honours, shall be placed in the First Division.

EXAMINATION FOR HONOURS

Any Candidate who has been placed in the First Division at the Second Examination may be examined for Honours in any or all the following subjects:

PHYSIOLOGY AND COMPARATIVE ANATOMY.
  Candidates may illustrate their answers by sketching the parts they describe.
SURGERY.
MEDICINE.
MIDWIFERY.

The Examinations shall take place in the week following the
SECOND EXAMINATION. They shall be conducted by means of
Printed Papers; but the Examiners shall not be precluded from
putting *vivâ voce* questions upon the written answers of the
Candidates when they appear to require explanation.

The Examinations shall be conducted in the following order:

Morning, 10 *to* 1.

Tuesday . . . Physiology and Comparative Anatomy.
Wednesday . Surgery.
Thursday . . Medicine
Friday . . . . Midwifery.

Afternoon, 3 *to* 6.

Tuesday . . . Physiology and Comparative Anatomy.
Wednesday . Surgery.
Thursday . . Medicine.

In determining the relative position of Candidates, the
Examiners shall have regard to the proficiency evinced by the
Candidates in the same subjects at the Pass Examination.

Candidates who pass the Examination, and acquit themselves to the satisfaction of the Examiners, shall be arranged
according to the several subjects and according to their proficiency in each; and Candidates shall be bracketed together,
unless the Examiners are of opinion that there is a clear
difference between them.

If in the opinion of the Examiners sufficient merit be evinced,
the Candidate who shall distinguish himself the most in Physiology and Comparative Anatomy, the Candidate who shall
distinguish himself the most in Surgery, and the Candidate who
shall distinguish himself the most in Medicine, shall each
receive an Exhibition of Fifty Pounds per annum for the next
Two Years, with the style of UNIVERSITY MEDICAL SCHOLAR.

Under the same circumstances, the First and Second Candidates in each of the preceding subjects shall each receive a Gold Medal of the value of Five Pounds.

Under the same circumstances, the Candidate who shall distinguish himself the most in Midwifery shall receive a Gold Medal of the value of Five Pounds.

DOCTOR OF MEDICINE

The Examination for the Degree of Doctor of Medicine shall take place once a year, and commence on the fourth Monday in November.

No Candidate shall be admitted to this Examination unless he have produced Certificates to the following effect:

1. Of having taken the Degree of Bachelor of Medicine in this University, or a Degree in Medicine or in Surgery at a University the Degrees granted by which are recognised by the Senate of this University*.

> Those Candidates who have not taken the Degree in this University shall produce a Certificate of having completed their Twenty-third year.

2. Of having attended, subsequently to having taken one of the above Degrees in Medicine,

a. To Clinical or Practical Medicine during Two Years in a Hospital or Medical Institution recognised by this University.

b. Or, to Clinical or Practical Medicine during One Year in a Hospital or Medical Institution recognised by his University, and of having been engaged during Three Years in the Practice of his Profession.

c. Or, if he have taken the Degree of Bachelor of Medicine in this University, of having been engaged during Five Years in the Practice of his Profession.

> One Year of attendance on Clinical or Practical Medicine, or Two Years of Practice, will be dispensed with in the case of those Candidates who at the Second Examination have been placed in the First Division.

3. Of Moral Character, signed by two persons of respectability.

These Certificates shall be transmitted to the Registrar at least fourteen days before the Examination begins.

The Fee for the Degree of Doctor of Medicine shall be Ten Pounds. No Candidate shall be admitted to the Examination unless he have previously paid this Fee to the Registrar. If a Candidate fail to pass the Examination, the Fee shall not be

---

* At present, all Candidates for the Degree of Doctor of Medicine must have previously obtained the Degree of Bachelor of Medicine in this University.

returned to him; but he shall be admissible to any subsequent Examination for the same Degree without the payment of any additional Fee.

The Examination shall be conducted by means of Printed Papers and *Vivâ Voce* Interrogation.

Candidates shall be examined in the following subjects:

> ELEMENTS OF INTELLECTUAL PHILOSOPHY, LOGIC, AND MORAL PHILOSOPHY.
>
> MEDICINE.

The Examinations shall be conducted in the following order:

By Printed Papers.

Morning, 10 to 1.

Monday . . . Elements of Intellectual Philosophy, Logic, and Moral Philosophy.

Candidates who have taken a Degree in Arts in this University, or in a University the Degrees granted by which are recognised by the Senate of this University, shall be exempted from this part of the Examination.*

Tuesday . . . Medicine

Afternoon 3 to 6.

Monday . . . A Commentary on a Case in Medicine, Surgery, or Midwifery, at the option of the Candidate.

Tuesday . . . Medicine.

By Vivâ Voce Interrogation.

Friday Morning, at 10.

Examinations on the Answers to the Printed Papers, and on the Commentaries: and Examination for a Certificate of Special Proficiency in Medicine, Surgery, or Midwifery, as determined by the Candidate's choice of the Case for commentary.

On Monday Morning in the following week the Examiners shall arrange in Two Divisions, each in alphabetical order, such of the Candidates as have passed. And a Certificate under the Seal of the University, and signed by the Chancellor, shall be delivered to each Candidate.

If in the opinion of the Examiners sufficient merit be evinced, the Author of the best Commentary on the Case in Medicine, the Author of the best Commentary on

---

* The Degrees in Arts of all Universities in the United Kingdom are recognised by the Senate for this purpose.

the Case in Surgery, and the Author of the best Commentary on the Case in Midwifery, shall each receive a Gold Medal of the value of Five Pounds.

Any Candidate may present a Thesis on a subject of his own choice. If in the opinion of the Examiners sufficient merit be evinced, a Gold Medal of the value of Ten Pounds shall be given to the Author of the best Thesis. The Examiners shall not be precluded from examining the Author on the subject of his Thesis.

If in the opinion of the Examiners sufficient merit be evinced, the Candidate who shall distinguish himself the most at the Examination for the Degree of M.D. shall receive a Gold Medal of the value of Twenty Pounds.

FRIDAY, November 22.—Morning, 10 *to* 1.

MIDWIFERY.

Examiner, Dr RIGBY.

1. Describe the prophylactic treatment of abortion.
2. What is the meaning of a Mole Pregnancy?
3. What are the sources of danger to the Child's life in face and nates presentations, and how would you act under such circumstances?
4. Give the diagnosis of true from false pains.

DOCTOR OF MEDICINE.

MONDAY, November 25.—Morning, 10 *to* 1.

ELEMENTS OF INTELLECTUAL PHILOSOPHY, LOGIC, AND MORAL PHILOSOPHY.

Examiner, Mr BURCHAM.

1. "There are and can be but two ways of investigating and discovering truth." What are these two methods, and what is the difference between them as regards the process of the mind?
2. One of the operations, which the word Induction has been used to designate, is "the *material* illation of a universal from a singular, as warranted either by the general analogy of nature or the special

presumptions afforded by the object matter of any real science." Show that this is the process of Bacon, and distinguish between it and the Aristotelian Induction.

3. Enumerate the causes or sources of the Idola Tribus, and the Idola Theatri.

4. Give Stewart's definition of consciousness. How, according to him, do we get the notion and conviction of our personal identity? Give any other solution of the question.

5. "It is to the use of artificial signs that we are indebted for all our general conclusions, and without it our knowledge would have been entirely limited to individuals." Give reasons for or against the above proposition.

6. "To what part of our constitution is the origin of our ideas of right and wrong to be ascribed?" How is this question answered by Hobbes, Cudworth, Locke, and Hutcheson? How do you answer it yourself?

COUSIN AND BUTLER

Examiner, Rev. H. ALFORD.

1. What, according to Locke, are the sources of all our ideas? How does he on his theory account for the ideas of space, time, infinity, personal identity, substance, causality?

2. What fundamental error pervades the whole of this part of Locke's system? How has it been carried out since his time, and by whom? What are, according to Cousin, its principal merits and demerits?

3. Give Cousin's refutation of Locke's view, that all judgment is founded on comparison.

4. What are the presumptions that we shall live after death, deduced from our present physical, intellectual, and moral state?

5. How is God's government by punishments justified by analogy? "In the natural course of things, virtue *as such* is rewarded, and vice *as such* punished." With what exception is this true? What may be inferred from the rule, and what from the exception?

6. Show that the government of God must be a scheme incomprehensible to us at present.

MONDAY, November 25.—Afternoon, 3 to 6.

COMMENTARY ON A CASE IN MEDICINE,
SURGERY, OR MIDWIFERY.
CELSUS *DE RE MEDICA*.

CASE IN MEDICINE.

Examiners, Dr. BILLING and Dr. TWEEDIE.

R. W. æt. 28, when first visited on the 20th of December, stated that he generally enjoyed good health, that his present indisposition, which was of three weeks' duration and had been preceded for ten or twelve days by slight cough, commenced by severe headache, loss of appetite, thirst, and chilliness succeeded by hot skin and tendency to sweating. The chilliness, which recurred every day at the same hour during the first week, had entirely disappeared. The bowels were at first confined, but for the last few days he had felt gripping pains in the abdomen, accompanied by frequent liquid evacuations from the bowels, and on the previous day he had voided by stool about half a pint of dark-coloured blood.

On the 21st he complained of epigastric tenderness and urgent thirst, the tongue was clean at the edges, brownish in the centre; but there was no headache and no pain of limbs; the pulse was only 76, there was little cough, the respiration was easy, the chest clear and resonant on percussion, and no kind of rale accompanied the respiratory murmur. His manner was calm, and though he replied to questions rather slowly, his intelligence was unimpaired. In the evening there were slight chills followed by heat of skin, but no sweating. The accession returned on the next and following days, but a little sooner. On the 25th there was no chill, but the diarrhœa, which had ceased since he was first visited, reappeared, and he had passed fifteen liquid stools. By the remedies administered, it was again restrained, though in the next few days it was evident that his powers were much depressed.

On the 1st of January he had frequent bilious vomiting, and passed from eight to ten small liquid dejections. Next day the expression of his countenance was visibly altered, the speech more slow, the pulse quicker, the skin moderately hot; there was cough accompanied with slight mucous expectoration. He had passed only three evacuations from the bowels during the day.

During the night of the 3rd and 4th, he suddenly experienced very severe pain in the hypogastrium, so severe as to cause him to utter loud shrieks; it continued with undiminished severity for an hour, and then abated considerably. When visited on the following day the belly was soft, and could be examined without apparently inducing much pain. The features however were much contracted, and his general powers very feeble: the pulse 110, respiration frequent, tongue clammy, and he complained of much thirst. On the morning of the 5th his countenance had become more animated, the whole body was covered with a profuse sweat, the abdomen was slightly tender, the tongue white, but his thirst had abated, and he had passed no stool for 24 hours. This apparently calm state was, however, interrupted in the evening by bilious vomiting. In the course of a few hours he complained of feeling very ill, and expired before midnight.

What was the nature of this disease?

What appearances would you expect to find on examination of the body after death?

How would you have treated this disease?

CELSUS.

Ubi verò febris aliquem occupavit, scire licet non periclitari, si in latus aut dextrum aut sinistrum, ut ipsi visum est, cubat, cruribus paulùm reductis; qui ferè sani quoque jacentis habitus est; si facilè convertitur, si noctù dormit, interdiù vigilat, si ex facili spirat, si non conflictatur; si circa ambilicum et pubem cutis plena est; si præcordia ejus sine ullo sensu doloris æqualiter mollia in utrâque parte sunt. Quòd si paulò tumidiora sunt, sed tamen digitis cedunt et non dolent, hæc valetudo, ut spatium aliquod habebit, sic tuta erit. Corpus quoque, quod æqualiter molle et calidum est, quodque æqualiter totum insudat, et cujus febricula eo sudore finitur, securitatem pollicetur. Sternutamemtum etiam inter bona indicia est, et cupiditas cibi vel à primo servata, vel etiam post fastidium orta. Neque terrere debet ea febris quæ eodem die finita est; ac ne ea quidem, quæ, quamvis longiore tempore evanuit, tamen ante alteram accessionem ex toto quievit, sic ut corpus integrum, quod εἰλικρινὲς Græci vocant, fieret. Si quis autem incidit vomitus, mixtus esse et bile et pituitâ debet, et in urinâ subsidere album, læve, æquale; sic ut etiam, si quæ quasi nubeculæ innatarint, in imum deferantur; at venter ei qui à periculo tutus est, reddit mollia, figurata, atque eodem ferè tempore quo secundâ valetudine assuevit, modo convenientia his quæ assumuntur.

Pejor cita alvus est: sed ne hæc quidem terrere protinùs debet, si matutinis temporibus coacta magis est, aut si, procedente tempore, paulatim contrahitur et rufa est, neque fœditate odoris similem alvum sani hominis excedit. Ac lumbricos quoque aliquos sub finem morbi descendisse nihil nocet. Si inflatio in superioribus partibus dolorem tumoremque fecit, bonum signum est sonus ventris indè ad inferiores partes evolutus; magisque etiam si sine difficultate cum stercore excessit.

CASE IN SURGERY.

Examiners, Sir STEPHEN L. HAMMICK and Mr HODGSON.

A gentleman, 65 years of age, of robust stature, but apparently of a phlegmatic temperament, of active habits, moderate in the use of fermented liquors, but addicted to much and good eating, rubbed the skin off the first joint of the left second little toe by wearing a tight boot. He suffered but little inconvenience for a week, when the toe became excessively painful and slightly inflamed. He thought he had an attack of gout, but he had never suffered from that disease, nor had he any other symptoms of it. In the third week from the time of the injury, the pain having continued unabated, the toe became dry, black, and in a gangrenous state to its metatarsal joint. The pain then ceased, and only a very slight degree of inflammation was observable over the metatarsus. The pulse at the wrist and the movements of the heart were feeble, but no unnatural sound could be detected in the precordial region. In the sixth week the inflammation extended over the metatarsus, accompanied with acute burning deep-seated pain in the foot generally, increased feebleness in the pulse at the wrist and at the heart, dry brown tongue, loss of appetite, and great prostration. In the seventh week gangrenous patches formed on the upper part and on the sole of the foot, preceded by slight swelling and vesications. The gangrenous patches extended, and in the eighth week reached to the ankle, having become partially detached in some places from which offensive putrid matter and sloughs were removed. The powers of the system gradually declined, low delirium and subsequently coma came on, and the patient died at the end of the eighth week from the time when he first perceived the abrasion of the toe.

In commenting on this case you are requested to describe the different forms of gangrene and their causes, symptoms and pathology, both with reference to remote organs and the state of the parts in which those conditions exist. You will also mention the modes of treatment, both general and local, which you would adopt, with your reasons for their employment.

CASE IN MIDWIFERY.

Examiner, Dr RIGBY.

Mrs. B., ætat. 42, mother of ten children.
July 18, 1850, eight months pregnant.
The membranes broke this morning, and there has been more or less discharge of blood; she was at a party last night and was much

oppressed by the heat of the weather; moreover she slipped down two or three days ago. Her bowels have been confined and unhealthy; they have been but partially rectified by medicine; the liver is torpid, and the tongue fissured.

Exam. per Vaginam.—The vagina is full of clots; the os uteri, which can barely be reached with the finger, is just beginning to dilate. No presenting part can be reached. Liquor amnii dribbles away; occasionally she has a slight pain, which increases the discharge.

July 19.—Slept well, had occasional slight pains all day; at about 6 P.M. they increased, and a hand could just be reached, the os uteri being about two-thirds dilated: both it and the os externum were very dilatable, and the attendant passed his hand with great ease; the other hand of the fœtus was found close by that which presented, but it was so soft and pliable that he did not feel certain until he had reached the elbow. On passing towards the abdomen of the child, he found the legs and brought one down; there was no pulsation in the cord, which passed between the child's legs. When the foot was brought into the vagina, it was left there until pains should come on. In half an hour they returned; more liquor amnii and blood followed; then came the nates of the child with the other foot; the arms, shoulders and head followed with great ease: the child was dead; there was some hæmorrhage afterwards, which was stopped by ergot, cold and pressure.

The Candidate is requested to make a few remarks on every practical point which may strike him.

TUESDAY, November 26.

MEDICINE.
Examiners, Dr BILLING and Dr TWEEDIE.

Morning, 10 *to* 1.

1. Explain the general principles on which the treatment of dropsy is founded.

2. Describe the different forms of small-pox. Sketch the symptoms, progress and treatment of confluent small-pox.

3. Explain how pneumo-thorax may arise. Give its physical signs and treatment.

4. Describe the anatomical characters, diagnostic symptoms and treatment of acute hydrocephalus.

Afternoon, 3 *to* 6.

1. Describe briefly the conditions of the heart (organic and functional) which are accompanied by abnormal sounds.

2. Enumerate the principal varieties in the expectoration in pulmonary diseases. What are the diagnostic indications to be drawn from each?

3. Sketch the causes, nature and treatment of anæmia.

4. Describe the anatomical characters, diagnostic symptoms and treatment of laryngitis.

FRIDAY, November 29, at 10 A.M.

EXAMINATION ON THE ANSWERS TO THE PRINTED PAPERS, AND ON THE COMMENTARIES.
By Vivâ Voce Interrogation.

Index